Mental Whiplash

THE QUIRKS THAT LIFE THROWS AT YOU

GAIL L. AUTHEMENT

Contents

Dedicated to my children,
Lenny and Renee

and my beautiful, wonderful grandchildren,
Sean, Isobel, and Luke

Who am I?

I'm your average normal person. At least I consider myself normal. What is normal, anyway? Someone I knew once said, "Normal is the setting of a washing machine." I graduated from the University of Florida with a degree in Special Education. Mostly, I am a graduate of the school of "Hard Knocks" with a degree in determination.

I am an introvert. I can be outgoing, depending on who I am around. Sometimes, I must take a step back and regroup. I regroup by being alone, which some people don't understand. In my younger life, I lived with a lot of severe depression that had a major impact on my life. I missed a lot of things. But I did the best I could. Keeping it inside was my way of coping with it. There was such a stigma attached to depression and I was embarrassed. That only served to push me further down. It was a vicious cycle. After four decades, I finally learned that no matter how bad it got, it wouldn't stay that way. I had some very joyful times, as well.

Since the first writing of this book, I have lost a lot of people dear to me. Among them are three cousins, my oldest brother, my mama, my son, and too many friends. This has been extremely hard for me. There is a huge hole in my heart. Right now, I am functioning less than adequately. There is no right or wrong way or specific time frame to go through the process. My grandchildren, who I live with and take care of while my daughter is working, provide a lot of love and distraction. A vast number of friends, family, and acquaintances have been kind and caring and many have me in their prayers.

Creativity has always been a part of me, and before arthritis developed, I painted with oils and acrylics, crocheted, did finger-weaving, made pottery, and many other crafts. I created and copyrighted a space doll called "Gail's Galaxy Gals and Guys". In addition, I performed as a professional clown, which brought me joy. Being a teacher was one of the best things I ever did, and it could be stressful, as well. In addition, singing has always been something I love to do. My granddaddy encouraged me to put my words to music when he read some of my poems. Writing for myself, my family, and students was fun, too.

My family heritage originates from France, Scotland, Ireland, and Native American ancestry. The names Authement, DuFrene, Lamb, Mulkey, and Kimbrell create a great stir in my heart. I am made up of good genes, and I am very proud of my heritage, although I don't know nearly enough about it. I used to ask my students if they had ever heard of the French-Indian War when they would be "off the chain". I would tell them they were just about to see me go on the war path if they didn't straighten up. They would get very still and quiet, and we could continue whatever subject or activity we were working on.

My kindergarteners loved to roll their pencils on their desk and talk during work time. To counteract the pencil rolling, I'd say, "Stop!" and tell them we were going to have a two minute timed pencil roll. They had to roll their pencils across their desks for two minutes but not let the pencils roll off their desks. As for the talking, we would have a two minute timed talking break. For the first few times I'd say this, they would look at me like I was crazy. At first, they would find the activity funny and laugh. When anyone asked if they had to roll their pencils or talk, I'd tell them yes, that they had to for the whole two minutes. If they stopped during the activity, I'd tell them they couldn't stop until the two minutes were over. When you are only five or six years old, two minutes isn't long unless you get tired of an activity. The negative behaviour decreased and positive behaviour increased. All of my kindergarteners were reading by the Christmas break, except for one. Children are amazing!

I have lived a very full life and although I have slowed down a great deal, I am thankful for all my accomplishments. I am especially thankful for my family and heritage. I have been blessed with amazing experiences, family and friends. Finally, my faith in God has sustained me in many ways.

Their Giving Heart

When I was a child, my parents would take us to Des Allemands, Louisiana almost every Christmas to see Daddy's mother and a lot of other family. Grandma Grace was a small lady and a precious one. She lived in a tiny house off a main road, which was beside the bayou and railroad tracks. She raised three of my cousins who were siblings. It was always a fun visit. Grandma cooked the best gumbo, beignets, and many more of our favorite foods. I never learned to drink the strong coffee, though! Best of all, I felt her great love for us, and we loved her very much. She spoke Cajun French and English – sometimes in the same sentence, which made it very interesting. A lot of times, we asked Grandma Grace to go with us when we went to various places in New Orleans. She usually stayed home to cook for us, while we were out enjoying ourselves. I never knew why she stayed in the kitchen long hours until I grew up. She was gracious, caring, kind, and always went the extra mile to see that we had the best of her heart and meals.

We would go to church on Sunday morning before we had to head back home. At Christmas time, the church always had stockings filled with candy for the children. They would have the children walk down the aisle to the front of the church to get the stockings. If they didn't expect us to be there, my cousin, Juanita, was told to share with me. After our favorite Sunday dinner, Juanita would get her stocking and she always offered me the first pick. She shared with me, never complaining. It was shared from her heart. Even as a child, I knew it was a sacrifice for her. Yet, she gave willingly and lovingly, so much like Grandma.

Visiting Grandma was always special. We enjoyed seeing her, and we visited with more of our family. I tried to learn the Cajun language but only learned a few words. One thing I did learn - one gesture leaves an impression that lasts a lifetime. Plus, it can make your heart grow bigger. These are some of the sweetest treasures and gifts.

Southern Life, Triumph and Tragedy

When I was about five years old, my family lived in Clinton, Mississippi – outside of Jackson. We lived on two acres of land and the house sat way back from the highway. In front of the house, there was a big gully that was supposedly dug during the Civil War. It was a fun place to live, and we were never bored as kids. Mama and Daddy would bring groceries home in boxes that we would break down and slide down the hill into the gully. We were surprised to have a blizzard one winter and our neighbors let us borrow their sleds to slide down the gully. Between the neighbors and us, there was a big canebrake. We kids were never allowed to go into it because Mama was afraid of snakes, and she said she couldn't come in to rescue us. We had several pecan and fruit trees that grew in the back yard. So, we could always have our pick of them. Plus, we had a lot of room to run and play. When Mary Ann Mobley was crowned Miss America, her family lived in Brandon, which wasn't too far away from us. I was thrilled and wanted to be just like her.

We kids made our own fun. The Wisteria vines were always a target to swing on, knowing we'd soon hear Mama yell, "Get off the Wisteria vines!" They were there, so what else were we to do, but swing on them? One afternoon, my older siblings and I decided to play "ghost". My brother decided to be the ghost and went inside the house. In a few minutes, he came out wearing a white sheet and said, "Whoooooooooooo!" I knew it was him but he was so convincing that I thought he was the real deal. My sister was standing beside me. I started screaming, clawing, and climbing up her like she was a tree! She yelled to my brother and told him to take the sheet off before I killed her. I don't remember us playing "ghost" ever again.

Daddy was so good to us and so smart; he could do anything. He made a seesaw for us and it was so much fun. It had a cement block on one end in case we played on it by ourselves. He would modify many of our toys so that they would work better and do more than they were supposed to do. We were fortunate that we had a daddy that loved to spend time on us. He spent a lot of time with us, as well.

We had a dog named Scout, and he and I spent a lot of time together outside. One day, he and I shared five hot dogs. Mama came out to see how I could eat that many hot dogs as little as I was and caught us! Scout and I were pals and he dragged me out of the highway one day when I decided to go across the busy road to play in the cemetery, and feed the ducks. He dragged me by my clothes into our yard and saved my life.

I loved standing at the end of our long driveway and watching traffic go by on Clinton Boulevard. I would always wait for one particular trucker and motion for him to blow his horn. One specific motorcycle police officer and I would always wave at each other. I was thrilled to have them as "friends". One afternoon, the officer decided to turn into the driveway to introduce himself. I was terrified and ran toward the house, screaming at the top of my lungs! I thought I was in trouble. He apologized and Mama laughed and explained what he had stopped for. He and I did talk, after Mama assured me that he was just being my friend and continued to wave every time he drove by from then on.

We had two very sweet cousins in Mississippi. Buddy and his family lived in Jackson and Theresa lived in Florence with her family. We were a trio and loved to spend time together in Florence. Our great grandmother had a real china tea set that we played with and we spent a lot of time together. The exterior of the house was made of stone and there was an old wishing well beside it. They had three ponds and we could fish. The inside of the house was intriguing because the hallway was surrounded by the bedrooms and a bathroom. The hallway had been turned into a library and there were a great many books neatly lined up on the shelves which went from the floor to the ceiling. I remember standing in there, gazing up at the shelves, and wondering what treasures those books held. I was too young to read most of them but how I longed to. Buddy got his first car while we lived in Clinton and he gave me a ride in it. He was so proud of his car and I was thrilled to ride with him. I felt special when I spent time with Buddy and Theresa.

When my family moved to Florida, I missed them greatly. I saw Aunt Lois and Uncle Willie, usually on a yearly basis but not my cousins. As we got older, we went in different directions and lost touch. I remember asking about them. Once, I was traveling by Greyhound Bus and stopped overnight. Aunt May took me to see Buddy's family. He had moved, married, and become a dentist. I didn't get to see him. Then, we went to Florence to see Aunt Lois. Aunt Lily was there. They called Theresa, who was married. She rushed over with her beautiful little girl, and we had a wonderful visit. That was the last time I saw them. I would keep up with them through Aunt May. I continued to look for Buddy and no one gave me any information on him. Aunt May told me that he was somewhere in Florida. I looked in phone books anytime I traveled in Florida, to no avail. It was like he had vanished into thin air, which was distressing for me. I have always needed my family, and I lost touch with Theresa again after the aunts and other family died.

Several years after social media became available, I started searching again. I continued searching anywhere I thought I could locate them. Finally, I came across a man on a social media with Buddy's last name. I was ecstatic to find a cover photo on his page, saw Buddy sitting at a table with his family. He was older but I knew it was him. He looked like his dad. I quickly sent a private message to the young man, explaining who I was, how long I had been hunting his dad, and asked him to put me in touch. I waited anxiously to hear back, realizing that he might never see it. But I hoped. Several weeks later, I saw that I had a message from him. He told me his dad didn't have an account but Carol, his mom did, and he gave me their cell phone numbers. He also told me that when he told his dad I had contacted him, that Buddy smiled. I then sent a message and friend request to Carol, who responded and I soon got to give Buddy a call. We got caught up on a lot of things. It turned out that he and Carol were both retired dentists, and had lived not too far from me in Florida. Also, he and Carol usually attended The Master's golf tournament in Augusta, Georgia. I was living in Augusta the first time we spoke, and we discovered that we had unknowingly been in the same city at the same time more than once! I had also traveled through the city where they lived many times. The golf tournament would be coming up soon and we made plans to meet. What a thrill to see each other and meet Carol! We had lunch together, reminisced, and planned to stay in touch.

Not long afterward, I found Theresa on social media. I was so joyful! We excitedly made plans to meet in Tennessee where Theresa lived. The trio would be together again for the weekend! How good could it possibly be? Just before we were to travel to Tennessee, my vehicle broke down. There was no way for me to get there. Buddy tried to console me and said that, although I couldn't be there this time, we would make plans for meeting again soon. He and Carol had a great visit with Theresa and her husband, Arthur. I got to enjoy the pictures they took and everything they told me about their visit.

We stayed in touch and learned more about each other's family. Buddy and Theresa have delightful families, and we are in touch through social media. Everything pointed to happy reunions and the makings of more warm memories. Sadly, our world would come crashing down when we lost our dear Buddy because of an injury to his foot. The injury developed into a massive infection, which tragically took him from us. I am very happy that we found each other again, even though we miss him greatly. We had just begun to reconnect and complete the circle. It is hard to understand why he was taken from us. However, I can still feel the love and warmth I felt when we all found each other again.

Mama had only one sibling, a sister, who had two daughters. Julie is older than me by three months. Although we have never had the privilege to see each other often enough, we have always had a special bond. They lived so far away, and when they did get to visit, it was always exciting. We had such fun together. Janet, who was younger and quiet, probably wondered what was wrong with us. I remember Janet's sweet smile when she would look at us without saying anything. It wasn't until we were grown, that Janet and I lived closer and got to know each other better. It's funny how life works out.

Julie and I were happy no matter what was going on. We could sit in the same room, read, and not say a word for a good while. We were content just being together. Usually when they would come down, Julie would bring a lot of clothes to me. I loved them because she gave them to me. She was so smart and did much better in school than I did. I always wanted to be as smart as she was. Plus, I wanted to be as tall and elegant as her, which never happened. However, our love for each other has always been there and always will be. There is such a happy warm place in my heart where I keep her and our memories.

Pen Pals

When I became a teenager, one of our church youth leaders decided that we teens from the different states that we lived in needed to get to know each other better. I lived in Florida and one of the pen pals he assigned me lived in Arkansas. Incredibly, this was the same small town that my grandmother was raised in. Connie and I had a lot in common and became close friends through correspondence.

When we were grown, we had the opportunity to meet in person. We met in Columbus, Georgia, where I had been born; spent the night with an older couple that we knew; and boarded the bus back to Arkansas. It was a long trip and made even longer when our bus broke down before we were barely out of town. It took about an hour to get another bus to get us. My two-year-old son made the wait interesting.

We had to go through Memphis, Tennessee where we'd have about an eight-hour layover and change buses. Ironic, because we weren't that far from our destination. Connie had a bad back and needed to rest. She said we needed to find a motel so we could sleep during the layover. I was paranoid to walk to a motel in that bad area of town around midnight. I was carrying my sleeping son wrapped in a blanket, and we carried our bags. What a sight we were.

We made our way into a dimly lit motel and got a room for the night that wasn't too far from the bus station. I'm sure that it wasn't a wholesome family place, and I was afraid. However, we were tired and needed to sleep that night. Although Connie's back was hurting, she insisted that my baby and I take the bed. She slept on the floor. That's a real friend. We woke up after a few hours and made it to the bus station in time the next morning. We spent a great week with Connie, and I got to meet her family. Although I wasn't ready to go home at the end of the week, it was time. We look back, reminisce, and laugh.

The next time we were able to see each other, she and her husband came to visit us in Florida. We are still hoping to meet again in person. But we cherish our memories until we can see each other again. We are very far apart in miles but close in thought and heart.

Teacher Strike

I was in eighth grade when teachers went on strike in Florida. Claude Kirk was governor of "The Sunshine State". Students went back to school about a month after we would have normally started, even though teachers were still on strike. The morning that we began that school year was utter chaos. We didn't know what to expect but we were happy to see our friends.

While we were standing and chatting with our friends, we saw a well-dressed man coming across the school yard with a couple of students following him. We wondered aloud who he was. As he walked, more students began to follow him. Someone said he was a detective, so our group decided to follow him. He turned around several times and found more students following him each time. We found out later that it was a parent hunting his son. I wish I knew what he was thinking with the crowd of students following him. In today's world, I think he would be a little frightened unless he was a very strong man.

When the bell rang, we began our school day. We only had one or two of our usual teachers who had to work to feed their children. I didn't know my best friend and neighbor was so scared of the chaos that she walked home. She went straight and told my mother that she'd better go check on me. So, Mama rushed to the school, only to find the mayor, who resembled "Boss Hogg", the corrupt sheriff on the TV show, "The Dukes of Hazzard". As Mama attempted to go through the entrance of the school, the mayor stretched out his arms and told her she couldn't go in. He didn't know Mama. She just stooped down and went under his arms and went in. She found out I was in Glee Club that period and went to check on me. She looked in the window of the door and saw me. I was singing, smiling, and looked as happy as I could be!

Unfortunately, we had to go to school for a month in the summer to make up the time that we had missed when the teachers were on strike. They returned which got us back on track. I, for one, was glad that we were together again. It was terribly hot, though. Those of us who were in the Glee Club were privileged to enjoy air conditioning from the only classroom with a window unit.

Trick-or-Treat

When we lived on Walton Street in Pensacola, we hung out with the neighbor kids, played outside, and rode bikes. Like so many kids, we complained about being bored when we ran out of fun things to do. One summer day, a bunch of us girls complained one time too many to Mama. She always had ideas to keep us busy. We should have known better. She got tired of us complaining and told us to get some paper bags and go trick-or-treating! We thought she was joking. We told her it was summertime, but she insisted. So we did. We got candy, pennies, or something from every house on the street! We were a close-knit neighborhood and knew everyone else. Several neighbors knew it was Mama's idea and would ask, "Your mama put you up to this, didn't she?" We would all laugh and go on our merry way. Mama was always up for something fun!

Believe it, Or Not

Grandmother wasn't very patient when she wanted or needed Mama and couldn't get her on the phone. We lived across the street and if this happened, Grandmother would call Bozo, our Boxer; pin a note to his collar; and tell him to take the note home to her. He'd immediately run home and get Mama's attention. He was proud of himself, and Grandmother was happy.

My younger brother and I used to play Monopoly, sitting on the floor. If Bozo was in the house, he would sit beside us. He was a pretty patient dog but if we didn't talk to him or pet him enough, he would get up and sit on our board, scattering everything and destroying our game. This happened so many times and it was hard to get him off our board. We got exasperated and came up with a good solution. We decided to teach him how to play with us. We'd give him his turn, take his huge paw, and make the dice roll. It actually worked! If we gave him his turn, he'd let us play and not sit on our game. If we forgot his turn he'd get up and sit in the middle of our board. He thought he was entitled!

He was quite a family member. When Daddy came home

from work he would go to wash up for supper. One afternoon, while Daddy was washing up, Mama fixed his plate and put it on the table. Bozo could smell it and decided he would eat it. When Daddy got to the table, there was Bozo, licking the plate clean. He got severely scolded. After that, Bozo decided since we sat in chairs, that was the proper way to eat and got up in Daddy's chair and ate while Daddy washed up. Mama and Daddy told him that he had to eat out of his own dish on the floor. Nice try, though! He never tried that again.

The Unthinkable

When my daughter was eight, I enrolled in a two-year college taking core classes. I attended classes while my children were at school and on Saturday mornings. Everything was going well, and I was enjoying my learning experience. Little did I know that things were about to change, and our lives would be turned upside down.

I arrived home one Saturday morning to be met by my thirteen-year-old son, who told me that something was wrong with his sister, who was eight years old. I rushed upstairs and found her in the bathroom, bleeding and in terrible pain. Immediately, I called our pediatrician, only to get another doctor, who was on call for him. He told me to monitor the situation and if the bleeding got worse to call him later in the evening. It got much worse, and I called. He had us meet him in the emergency room. We were so afraid. She was in so much pain when the doctor examined her that I had to hold onto her arms to keep her from pushing him away. He couldn't pinpoint where the blood was coming from but told us to watch her that night and to call him the next morning if it hadn't subsided.

The bleeding progressed and the pain became more intense

throughout the night. Our worry grew and I called the doctor the next morning. He told me to get her to the hospital, and to bypass the emergency room, and to go straight to the exam room. By that time, Renee was hemorrhaging. There were no immediate answers, so she was admitted to the hospital. They would have to do more exams and testing to know what to do. Testing and prodding, they did.

Watching your child suffer is one of the worst things a mother has to endure. Renee wanted answers as well. We had none. My heart felt like it would break watching her suffer like she did. I watched her turn pale as she lost more blood. I was watching life drain from my child. They asked me to stay and help hold her so they could do the exams and some of the testing. She would fight them with all her strength. With tiny rolling veins and reactions to IVs, they'd have to start over numerous times. If I could have taken her place, I would have.

No answers came in the next several days and I continued to watch her life drain out of her and the pain become excruciating. Watching her suffer in this way was horrible. As they gave her more blood to keep her alive, she continued to lose it. All I could do was stay with her, talk to her, and pray. There was no way to comfort her. At one point, she looked at me and weakly asked, "Mommy, why do I hurt like this?" I had no answer but out of my mouth came, "I don't know, baby, but Jesus does." Then, she asked, "But why would Jesus let me hurt like this?" Again, something in me said, "I don't know, but maybe it is so that you will someday have compassion for others."

Renee was put in ICU to monitor her. I could hear several doctors discussing her condition. They didn't know I could hear them, but I could tell they were baffled. Finally, I heard one of them say he thought it could be some condition that I didn't hear clearly. In just a little while, another doctor had been called in from Nemours Children's Hospital and introduced himself. He explained that the lining of her intestines was inflamed and swollen. He said he needed to use a scope to check her small intestines as high as possible. After he did the colonoscopy, he told us the diagnosis was Ulcerative Colitis. Her intestines were ulcerated, and it would take over a year to heal completely.

Renee was soon rolled back into the ICU and hooked up to several IVs. She was on about 10 different medications. Scary. However, within twenty minutes of the IV drips, I could see life coming slowly back into my baby's body. Her color returned, and she began to move around as the pain subsided. When she began to bounce around, I didn't tell her to be still or be quiet. I was so thankful to see her alive. We had quite a journey and her diet was strict; she was on several medications for quite a while. She went through a lot of ridicule because of the Prednisone she had to take, making her gain a lot of weight. It was next to impossible to find clothes that fit. We had to coach and encourage her daily and it was a challenge. But she was a trouper and made it through to a healthier lifestyle. Today, she is a strong person and is in a field to help others find their way through challenges.

Catching a Greyhound

Having parents that always made sure we did wholesome happy things as a family through the years, one of those special things was when we went fishing. We fished on what was then called "The World's Longest Fishing Pier". A new bridge was built over Pensacola Bay and the old bridge was divided in half for people to fish. It was a lot of fun fishing with our family.

Daddy made sure we got a good spot and gave us a lot of instructions and help. Mother made sandwiches and packed food and drink for us. I was a little kid, but I ate like I was ravenous. Daddy always baited my hook and took the fish off the hook for prissy little me. I didn't want to get my hands messy. Daddy stopped more times than I could count to help me. He had patience like no other one I know. He never complained. Plus, he was overjoyed when we caught anything and bragged on us joyfully.

Now, the new bridge wasn't that many feet away from the pier. We could watch the traffic as it went by. One day, Daddy was teaching me how to cast my new rod and reel. After I got the hang of it, I began casting it myself. I was so proud of myself. I caught some fish. Soon, I threw my line out and I heard a clinking sound, and my hook was caught on something. We looked and saw it had caught on a Greyhound bus just as it broke my hook. Daddy gave me the regular fishing pole to use the rest of the day. It is still fun to repeat this true fishing tale.

Don't Take Life for Granted

It was the last full day of October. We had a wedding to attend in Pensacola. My nephew was getting married, and we were going to travel over on Saturday morning from Jacksonville, the day of the wedding. I had planned carefully so that everything would go smoothly. It would be a day of joy, a day of celebration, and a day of making memories. To help preserve the memories of this special day, I had promised to videotape the wedding. A wedding is a new beginning. Little did we know what was in store. A new beginning would happen for me, too.

As the day of the wedding drew closer, my daughter asked to stay home. She was scheduled to work that weekend. I wanted her to go with us. To no avail, no matter how much I tried to convince her to ask for time off, the more determined she was to stay home. I felt uneasy leaving my teenage daughter, but it became apparent that we would all be miserable if she were forced to go. So, I arranged for her to stay with my younger brother and his family, who lived not too far from us. She promised to abide by their rules.

However, my uneasiness only grew in the days before we

were to leave. I thought it was due to allowing her to stay in town. By Friday, a feeling settled over me like a dark cloud. It hung over me all day, growing more ominous as the day wore on. I told myself that I was only being paranoid; that there was nothing to worry about. As usual, I went to see my nephews and their mom that afternoon. As we talked, I told her that I didn't want to go to Pensacola. She looked surprised and said, "You? You don't want to go?" She knew that I always wanted to be at family gatherings. I had never missed an opportunity to be in the mix whenever possible. It renewed me. She said she couldn't believe I didn't want to go. I told her that I wanted to be in Pensacola, but I didn't want to travel. By that night, the uneasiness had blossomed into dread.

However, the next morning, my husband and I had the van packed and we left the house around 5:30 a.m. I was happy that I had everything ready early so that we could have time to relax before the wedding. I was happy that I would be seeing the rest of my family. I leaned my seat back and fell asleep. After a while, Roy woke me up and asked if I wanted to stop for coffee. I agreed. I wanted him to be alert to drive. We stopped at a convenience store and got coffee. This was the first time I had ever seen flavored coffee creamer. As we got back into the van and pulled out, I mentioned that this was the best cup of coffee I'd ever had. It was just what I needed, and I savored it. I began to relax. Rain began to fall heavily and the cloud over my head grew. I'd never liked to travel in the rain, especially the kind we were now in. I sipped my coffee, my bare feet propped up on the dashboard. Having just been released that week from five weeks of physical therapy, due to an earlier auto accident, I would be so glad to get to Pensacola!

Strangely, a calm feeling washed over me as the rain beat down on the van and we hit the water that had quickly accumulated on the overpass. Then my worst fear came true. We swerved on the overpass, barely missing another vehicle. By now, our thoughts were racing as we headed off the interstate. Suddenly, it felt like we were on a wild roller coaster ride as the back of the van lifted off the pavement and we were airborne. The van rolled over three times as we sailed down the embankment. I thought we were going to die when we crashed. There was no way we would survive.

It is amazing how many things went through my mind. Pictures of my life flashed around me. I thought of those we would be leaving behind. I even thought about my cup of coffee and wondered when it would burn me as it spilled. I heard glass breaking next to me; felt the dark rainy morning air rush inside the van. What would our children do? Our son was grown and could take care of himself, but our daughter was still a minor. The wedding would go on without us. When were we going to crash? I prepared for impact with the trees that were impossible to miss. It was still dark, not quite seven o'clock. Who would find us? How long would it take to discover us down at the bottom of the embankment? What was that bright light I suddenly saw? When would we stop turning over and over? Where were the trees? What was that loud noise? Things were flying all through the van. What a mess this would be to clean up. Why didn't someone who saw us sailing over and down the embankment stop and help? Was that some wild animal that just brushed against me?

Just as quickly as it had begun, it stopped. It was still dark and neither of us could see anything. It took a few minutes to gather my senses. I finally heard Roy moving. He spoke first, asking me if I was alright. I said I was and asked if he was. He told me he was and told me that he couldn't find his glasses or cell phone. I realized that I was stuck upside down in my seat belt and couldn't get out. I was on my head with my neck bearing the weight that the seat belt could not bear. I had the strange sensation that I was turned around in my seat and sitting on the dashboard. I wasn't, I was disoriented.

There are many things in life that we don't understand. I am still amazed that we were alive and able to walk away. I am in awe that if the crash had happened any other way, we would not have survived. I sustained a Traumatic Brain Injury, Post Traumatic Stress, and short-term memory issues. My life was totally changed forever. I looked the same, but I wasn't. I have short-term memory issues and had to go through over two years of cognitive therapy. I had to learn strategies to help me get through simple everyday tasks and more complicated tasks as well. Keeping a notebook with me to write down everything became a must. If I forgot my notebook, or forgot to write tasks and directions down, it would create chaos for me. I struggled through conversations and forgot conversations. I forgot things that I did and forgot to do things. My already low self-esteem crumbled, and I would "beat myself up" mentally.

We did get to Pensacola in a rental - a small red truck, which was the only thing the little rental company had on a Saturday morning. I was in shock, and we didn't tell anyone what had happened until we arrived and visited with family for a while. I did get to film the wedding, standing on a very painful swollen toe, and in a chair to make sure I got everything filmed.

We were alive! I don't take life for granted. Anything can happen anytime, anywhere. All of my life previously I had asked myself why I had been born and if I had a purpose. I realized I am here for a reason, and I do have a purpose.

My Kids, The Pranksters

One day, after work I was very tired and decided that I would pick up my kids from my parents' house, and drive through a fast-food place so that I wouldn't have to cook dinner. I gathered up their things, told them to get into the car while I went to speak to a neighbor for a few minutes. Earlier, the child next door who played with Renee had asked to come home with us. I explained that she couldn't come on a school night, but she could come on the weekend. When I got back, my kids were both in the car and I told them we were going to stop for burgers. They were excited and both cheered. I heard Renee whispering in the back seat and saw Lenny smiling in the front seat. I asked them what they were whispering about but got no reply. I was tired and didn't pursue the question again.

It took less than 10 minutes to get to the drive-through. I ordered and paid for our food. Pulling up to the next window to get the order, I handed Lenny his first. Then, I handed Renee's to her over the seat. As I turned around, a little angelic face from my floorboard said, "I'm hungry, too." It was Amanda, the neighbor child who I'd told that she couldn't go home with us that night.

I was stunned. I got hysterical, both laughing and crying at the same time. The young girl who had handed me our food had seen the child on my floorboard and wondered what was wrong with me. All I could think of was that I was going to get arrested for kidnapping. I couldn't think rationally. I just knew that I had to take Amanda home quickly before they missed her. I drove her home and they had just missed her.

I remember pulling her out of the car and carrying her to her house because she wouldn't go willingly. I got her into her house and explained what had happened. Everyone laughed except for me. I was still in an irrational state of mind. It didn't occur to me that they would understand because we were friends. I was shaking. It took a while before I let her come home with us because I would start shaking when I saw her. I was able to laugh eventually, and she came home with us again.

A Two-Fold Character Trait

A characteristic can have more than one side, and the strongest one that runs in my family is two-fold. It has been passed down from generation to generation and is stubbornness. We'd rather have our say about what we think as much as we love to eat. Stubbornness is ironic. It is a strong trait. It has gotten me in trouble, especially when I was growing up. It can create many problems. However, the flip side is determination.

While stubbornness can create problems and produce a stalemate, or rift, in certain situations determination can solve many things. I saw how my grandmother and mother were determined and solved things. My mother always took negatives and turned them into positives because of her determination. She survived two forms of cancer and handled life because of determination. If I can be only half the person my mother was, I will get through anything.

Several times, when I went through the doors of the nursing home to see her, different ones would tell me my mother was stubborn. I would reply, "Yes, but the flip side of stubbornness is determination and that is how she has survived this long." They would always agree. Determination will carry you through many challenging times.

When I was in college, I thought that I would never pass algebra. But I refused to give up. Many times I wanted to but I knew I had to pass it to reach my goal of teaching. My friend Linda told me once that I had taught her not to give up. Wow! I was surprised. I had never thought I'd have that kind of influence on anyone. I had told Linda that I would conquer it because I would not let it conquer me. I was determined and conquered it.

I'm not proud of my stubbornness, but since it is two-fold, I am proud of my determination. It is necessary in many challenging situations in life. There will always be challenges, difficulties, and mountains to climb but on the flip side of stubbornness, determination will get me what I need.

<h1 style="text-align:center">Slips and Trips</h1>

Several times in my life I have fallen off of my own two feet. You probably have, too. I had a concussion when I was a kid. I fell backwards onto the concrete when a jump rope was pulled out from under me. I also dove onto the floor in the dark bedroom, forgetting the furniture had been moved that day. I should have turned the light on. When I traveled as a merchandiser on two of the biggest routes in the state, I was cleaning out my van and reorganizing my work materials. I lost my balance, tripped over a box, and hit the pavement. My glasses broke and the right lens cut into my eyebrow, requiring stitches.

I am probably the only person who has tripped over a speed bump as I was walking home one night. As I tried to look up from the ground, I spotted something pink and wrinkled to the right of my head. My head was hurting and I was frightened. Plus, I was irrational and afraid to move. I thought it was a chunk of my brain lying on the ground! If I moved my head much, I might lose more of my brain. However, I couldn't get up by myself. I slowly crawled over to my friend's car while my daughter helped me up. I had tried to pull up on the bumper but couldn't. I thought about my brain on the ground as we were slowly inching to our house and I was surprised that there wasn't an enormous amount of blood dripping down my face. Suddenly, I realized that my paper tissue wasn't in my hand. That was what was on the ground and not my brain! I was relieved and began to black out. I sat down to stop the blackness, nausea, and whirling. Soon, a friend riding on his golf cart came by, took us home and got me into the first chair in the den. I had a big purple eye by the next day but my brain was still in my head!

I lose my balance several times a day and walk into walls and furniture. I fall. A few months ago, I tripped over one of my granddaughter's toys and my toe got stuck. Trying to get it unstuck, I couldn't keep my balance and fell. Pain! My little toe had bent so far that it broke. It still swells with pain because of the location of the break. Don't panic, though! I am under the care of a neurologist and will be seeing a neurosurgeon very soon. I will also go back to physical therapy.

Christmas In March

Christmas is a time for family, a time we celebrate the Christ Child's birth. Our family always tried to be together for Christmas and we would travel to be together. As the family grew, it became more of a challenge to get everyone together. One particular year, we were determined to be together. My granddaddy wouldn't be with us much longer since he had multiple myeloma, cancer of the bone marrow and was bed-fast. So, we agreed to meet in March at my grandparents' house in Perry, Georgia.

We didn't think of March being right for a Christmas celebration, but we knew we would enjoy being together and it gave us something to look forward to. Mama was fun and she promised the kids in the family that there would be snow in March in Central Georgia! We laughed. It was a crazy idea that there would be snow there. But all the grandkids believed her.

After we all arrived, we were sitting there involved in an activity when someone looked out of the window and hollered, "Snow!" We all looked out the window and saw white flakes of ice and snow. One of the kids said, "Granny promised it would snow and it is!" Yes, it was snowing!

It was a wonderful Christmas celebration and we all got to enjoy Granddaddy's last Christmas together. It was a joyful happy time. How it snowed that time of year there, none of us know. However, it was like a miracle and the kids, who already thought their granny could make miracles happen, came to believe that she could do anything for them. Miracles do happen and one just might be right around the corner!

Working at The Bank

As my children got to a certain age, I decided it was time for me to go back to work. I got hired as a temporary clerical worker at a Florida bank, filling in for the secretary who was out on medical leave. This was in a state-wide credit card division. When the secretary returned, I was placed in billing and customer service for the cardholder department. I enjoyed the work and got to know all the major cities in Florida and the addresses of the banks. When I would travel, I would know where our branches were and look for the location if we were on the right road or highway.

In the cardholder department there was a lady who was comical. She didn't mean to be - she just was. She was forever saying things that made us laugh. One day, one of our co-workers got sick and fainted on the floor. When she came to, she asked, "Where am I?" The funny employee said, "You're on the floor!" Another day, we heard her answer the phone. We heard her but we couldn't hear the customer. She said, "No, this is the bank." "You have what?" "No sir, I can't send anyone to get the alligator out of your yard, this is the bank!"

After a while, I got bored working in the cardholder

division, and I asked to work in the merchant division. I got the job before too long. In that position, I got to know branch managers, loan officers, and some of the bank presidents around the state of Florida. My position was to help them program the point-of-sale terminals and train them on how to use them. I also had the responsibility to read credit reports in order to approve merchants' accounts for accepting credit cards. If approved, I would order the charge plates and mail them to the branches around the state. Finally, I studied the daily merchant reports to check for fraudulent charges.

One day, my supervisor came to my desk and asked me to please speak with Mr. Gucci. Yes, Mr. Gucci. We had all his store accounts, since he had some stores in Florida. I was intimidated and asked why I had to talk to him. She told me that they couldn't reason with him. He was used to getting what he wanted because of his vast wealth and power. We weren't able to accommodate him because we did not have the capability to do so. He was truly angry and berating the department chairperson and no one could reason with him.

I agreed to take the call. I had no choice, but I was very unnerved and intimidated. I listened to him go loudly and angrily about how he wanted us to accommodate him, and we were refusing. I wanted to bring him around to save the account and get him to understand that what he was requesting was not in our capability. I understood that he did not intend to accept what we had told him. I finally told him that I understood what he was saying, and that I wished we could accommodate him, and that I would feel the same way if I were him. Each time he ranted about what he wanted, I repeated how I understood how he felt and that I would be upset, too. He finally calmed down. He calmed down enough to finally say that he understood where we were coming from as I continued to repeat myself. We needed his account and we had bent over backwards each time previously, but this time we weren't able to. The conversation between the two of us lasted about thirty minutes and ended on a pleasant note. He had finally agreed to do things our way, thinking it was his idea! You would have thought that I was one of his best friends as we wrapped up our conversation and anytime that I had to speak with him afterwards, he was pleasant. After the incident was over, my supervisor and the department chairperson called me into her office and thanked me for a job well done. I asked them why they had given me the responsibility of dealing with him. They told me that it was because they knew I could handle it and help him to see it our way, and they thanked me profusely for saving the account.

Mama and Daddy

My siblings and I had the best parents. They loved us beyond measure. With all the love they had in their hearts, I wouldn't think that they would have any room left over for any other children. However, they were always taking in more children when the Children's Services called on them. Not only did they take children in, but also took in adults with children who needed a temporary place to stay. We, their kids, never knew how many extras would be there until we got home from school. But we thrived in our environment. It was normal for us.

Two of our cousins lived with us a couple of times and they were like siblings to us. Richard was only eleven months older than me, so he and I bonded closely. I gave that poor boy much trouble and got him in trouble as well, until Mama caught on. For instance, one day Mama heard me calling, "Mama, make Richard stop!" I was much smaller than him and Mama thought he was picking on me. When she looked out the back door, she found me sitting on him and hitting him. He was holding his hands over his head to keep me from giving him some hard punches. He knew he wasn't allowed to hit me. I couldn't deliver enough hard punches with his hands in the way. Poor Richard!

Now, among the foster children there were Tommy and Kenny. Tommy was just a tiny baby and so small that he could be diapered with a cloth no bigger than a handkerchief and could fit in a coffee can. Tommy grew strong and healthy as Mama and Daddy nourished and loved him. Kenny was just a little younger than I was, and he was my playmate. I remember a little wagon that we took turns pulling each other around in. I also remember being very protective of him as well. We spent hours together while my two older siblings were at school. He was a beautiful little boy with blonde hair and glorious blue eyes. I can still see him clearly in my mind and wonder about him; where he is, and hope he is well and happy.

After a few years, Children's Services found permanent homes for Tommy and Kenny. We were heartbroken. They were a big part of our family. I spent about thirty years of my adult life searching for Kenny, since I was so close to him. He was my little brother and best friend, and I needed him. I stopped looking for him, knowing that if it is meant to be, it will be. However, my eyes and ears are always open to the possibility of running into him somehow, someway. Once when my vehicle broke down, a man named Kenny stopped to help me. Yes, I asked him where he was from and if he had been adopted. He said no. I was disappointed.

Another time, there were two more brothers who came to live with us for a short while. As a matter of fact, they came more than once. They had run away from every foster home they had lived in, and they would make a dash for our door, run out of our yard and down the street. My siblings and I would chase them and bring them back home. I don't think I was supposed to be part of the rescue, but I wanted to be. I am sure that I was in it for the excitement. There was never a dull moment when these boys were with us.

Yes, Mama and Daddy had a lot of room in their hearts and truly loved each other. They were always there for us and each other, no matter what. They stuck by and treasured each other throughout their lives. Knowing a lot of what they went through makes it even more precious to remember. I am sure they sacrificed much for us and them and the many others they gave to.

We didn't have a lot of money; however, I didn't have an inkling about it until I was in high school. That didn't matter to me. We had plenty to eat and enough clothes to wear. We had good doctors when we needed them. Daddy worked hard in construction and Mama stayed home with us when we were young. Those were the days when men were supposed to provide for their families and most women worked at home raising the children, cooking, cleaning, and taking care of the home. We were healthy, wholesome, and happy children. Mama's parents lived close by, so we had their help when needed, too.

Now, Mama and Daddy were always up for fun and loved to take us kids places to see. There were plenty of free things and places back in the fifties and sixties and we never lacked places to go and enjoy. We would go to the airport to watch the planes come in and go out. Then, the passengers loaded and unloaded a little way from the building and walked up or down stairs to or from the plane to the building. We would go to the beach in the summer and go fishing in the summer and winter. We would fish on an old bridge that had been divided in half when the new Pensacola Bay bridge was built.

Also, I got to ride an elephant and Daddy took me to meet Sky King, Tarzan, and Elsie the Borden's cow. We all enjoyed riding the trolley in New Orleans and went to the New Orleans Zoo and to the zoo in Jackson, Mississippi. I still love zoos and seeing the animals. My sister told me that I got that from Daddy.

He went to the zoo during his lunch hour to see the animals sometimes.

We didn't grow up with a TV, but we didn't need one. Mama and Daddy always made sure that we had wholesome experiences at home and away from home. Mama sent a bunch of us girls, including neighbor girls, trick-or-treating in the middle of the summer when we complained that we were bored. Daddy hooked up an outside speaker to the house at Christmas time so that Christmas music was played for us and our close neighbors! No one complained so it must have been accepted - or they didn't want to hurt Daddy's feelings. He was a kind man. We were close-knit neighbors, though, and anyone could have said how they felt. We all knew each other and looked out for each other. When we kids got into trouble with a neighbor, we knew we would get into trouble with our parents. That probably kept us from getting into a lot of things. Mama and Daddy were strict, but they were also fun.

One Christmas, one of the neighbors gave me a bicycle they had outgrown. I knew ahead of time and was excited. Daddy wanted to repaint it so that it would look new to me. He asked me how I wanted it painted. I told him that I wanted it blue with three white diamond shapes down the center bar. He did it exactly as I asked. I was so proud of that bike and even more proud that Daddy painted it just for me!

Mama and Daddy did so much for us. They took little things and made them big for us. They took old things and made them new. They took us to church, taught us morals and values and how to treat our fellow men, women, and children. They taught us that all people are created equal in God's sight and to treat others as we want to be treated. They loved us and sacrificed a lot of their time and needs for us after we were grown, too. If we got really sick or hospitalized, Daddy would put Mama on a plane or drive her to us. Our parents were the most selfless people I have ever known.

When Mama had colon cancer surgery, she was recuperating in ICU when Daddy decided to put a new roof on the house. He wanted it done while she was in the hospital so that the noise wouldn't disturb her. He went and chose some samples of shingles and wanted Mama's approval before he did it. My sister and I were in the waiting room when he came back to the hospital during visiting time. He told us that he was going to show them to Mama. We looked at each other and thought he had to be kidding but he wasn't. He actually took them into her ICU room and got her approval. She approved quickly because she didn't care in the shape she was in. Daddy was happy and had the new roof done right away!

When Mama had breast cancer surgery, Daddy changed the sheets on the bed before she came home that had two different patterns of flowers and two different colors. It was hideous. I gently told him that Mama wouldn't like that combination and he asked me why. I told him the sheets didn't match and she would fuss. He said, "My goodness!" and he changed the sheets.

My daddy could fix and repair anything and was frequently tinkering with things like watches, electronics and anything else that had parts. He could repair cars and other mechanical things and did so more times than I can count. One Christmas, my younger brother and his friend across the street each got gas-powered toy airplanes. The little boys got to fly them for a while until the dads took them for themselves. The dads had a fun time until they literally ran into each other. They had to be taken to the hospital with injuries. One broke a bone! When they were asked what had happened, they said they had a plane crash!

Now, Daddy had the "patience of Job" when I needed help with my homework. Mother could help me with projects and anything but math homework. She would always give me the correct answer but I had no idea how she knew it was right. I would tell her I had to know how she got the answer because I had to show my work. But she didn't know how she got the answer. She just pulled it out of her head. Therefore, Daddy got stuck helping me with math and knew how to show me how to do the work, helping me to understand it. He always guided me along until I understood the concept. How he had the patience, I don't know. It had to be love.

Mama and Daddy went through a lot of challenges throughout their lives together and it strengthened their love for each other. They were best friends and confidants and complimented each other. Mama was easily excitable, talkative, and demonstrative. Daddy was calm, quiet, and thoughtful. However, when he had something to say, it was important. They were both highly intelligent. When Mama was concerned about us when we were grown, she would ask him what they should say. Daddy would say, "Hon, we can't tell grown kids what to do. They're going to do what they want to." Mother would say, "You're right, Honey." That was that.

After Daddy died so unexpectedly, it was hard for Mama. Her best friend was gone, and she began to exhibit subtle signs of dementia. I just thought it was the grieving process. A lot of it was but she was heartbroken and I think that is why she developed dementia. Her only sister passed away suddenly a few months after Daddy did and the dementia developed into Alzheimer's. She had to be put in a nursing home because I couldn't be with her while I was working and she fell too many times. I couldn't pick her up from the floor. When I visited her, she often told me she had talked to Daddy that day. That made me happy because it made her happy. To her, it was real. If one has dementia or Alzheimer's, it is comforting to have the love of your life by your side, whether real or imagined. To her, it was real. Who can argue with that? Besides, it is not appropriate or conducive to argue with an Alzheimer's patient. Their delusions and hallucinations are real to them. Mama died in December of 2022 and I know they are in Heaven, together again.

Granddaddy and Grandmother

Both of my grandparents were serious people but had a great sense of humor. Grandmother's mother died in childbirth while giving birth to her younger sister. It left a mark on her, as did her abusive father. He took everything out on her when he was angry. He remarried a really nice woman who loved both girls and they loved her. She was good to them and for them. However, her father divorced her and married another woman who did not like or tolerate the girls. How sad.

Grandmother, like children of that era, had to work in the fields, picking cotton and potatoes. It was hard, back-breaking work and the summer sun was hot. One of the neighbors was abusive to her as well. Grandmother told me that she decided to take matters into her own hands one day and she waited patiently until the man went into the potato house. She said she went quickly and quietly shut the door and locked it from the outside. It took a while for anyone to find him locked inside and let him out. When Grandmother laughed about something, she really laughed about it. She said she was happy that she had paid him back, laughing so hard that it made me laugh. I am sure that she paid a price for her deed. As she told me the story when I was a child, I could picture the scene from her description as if I had been there.

Now, Granddaddy and I were always playing pranks on each other. We kept Grandmother busy trying to keep us in line. Sometimes, she laughed at many of our antics. On the other hand, she would just shake her head. As we played our pranks, we got better at them. It could not have been more fun if we had won blue ribbons for our shenanigans. We used great precision and stealth, and Grandmother would not find out until the victim discovered the deed.

One particular prank was when Granddaddy removed the 8x10 framed photograph of my boyfriend from my dresser and hid it. Sometimes, he would turn it upside down. One day, as expected, it was missing. I looked all over my room and in drawers and could not find it for two days. I finally asked him where it was and he told me that I would never find it this time. I continued to look and each time I asked him about it, he would repeat that I would never find it. Finally, as I walked into my room again, I turned on the light and looked up. There it was! He had put it up in the ceiling light cover! Good one! Of course, now I had to top him.

The next day, I topped him! I pulled the ultimate prank on him, much to his and Grandmother's dismay. It took careful planning and stealthy work so that Grandmother wouldn't discover it before Granddaddy became the victim. I was successful. I anxiously waited for him to get home from work. He went into the bathroom, and I waited just outside the closed door. It happened just as I had carefully planned. I heard him exclaim, "Oh, my goodness gracious!" and I ran down the hallway laughing so hard! When Grandmother heard the commotion, she rushed to see what had happened. Granddaddy had opened the bathroom door and was standing in shock and disbelief. The bathroom floor was wet, and it was a big mess! I was the only one laughing. My payback was the end of pranks for a while. It was a few weeks before my grandparents could laugh about it. I am sure I was watched carefully afterwards and didn't have a chance to play any more pranks. We reinstated our pranks but they weren't as intense for Grandmother's sake.

My grandparents were good people. I miss them a lot. Granddaddy let me help him with his work once because I kept begging him. He was a master tile setter and was very particular about it. He was an artist, creating precision mosaics and patterns on floors and walls. He also did terrazzo floors. His work was beautiful. He was a great encourager as well. In addition, he was a loyal friend and family member.

Grandmother was an immaculate housekeeper and an incredible cook. To top it off, she did her housework in nice dresses, hose, and high heels. It was said that her floors were so clean that you could eat off them! She was as particular at home as Granddaddy was at his work. Grandmother loved to adopt stray dogs and cats and they loved her as much as she loved them. She even tamed squirrels to eat out of her hands. She named her favorite one Buddy and when they moved from Pensacola to Charleston, S.C., Buddy moved with them. My grandparents were grandparents to all the children in the neighborhood, who called them Grandmother and Granddaddy like we did. Oh, the incredibly wonderful memories remain in my heart. My grandparents.

Volunteering with AmeriCorps®

When I worked and attended classes at the Junior College of Jacksonville, an opportunity arose in which I could serve with AmeriCorps®, the national service corporation. This opportunity was too great to pass up, even though I was already working three other part-time jobs. It was a co-op between our two-year college and a four-year college close by. Dr. Cohen was the department chair and my supervisor in the Social and Behavioral Sciences department. She was over the project at our college. It was easy for me to sign up for the experience. I took on a two-fold position. One was as the payroll clerk and the other was part of a team volunteering in inner-city schools. We worked closely with Cities in Schools and the COPS Unit, which made for a well-rounded experience.

It turned out to be one of the best experiences I ever had and certainly gave me the best hands-on training to prepare me to be a teacher. We worked in classrooms with teachers and with small groups of students, as well as doing anything we were called to do. Our responsibilities could change daily and we were very eager to serve and prepare for our future teaching experience.

My first assignment was with a teacher who was a rather

bizarre person. She was a good educator some days but had poor classroom management skills. The reason was that she was an alcoholic and actually drank on the job. She would disappear for a long while, leaving me with her students. I did the best I could and soon learned how to teach them and keep them on task and in order. Then she would return, and the students would go back into utter chaos. Now, I was unaware that when she would leave the classroom, she would go out to her car, and drink alcohol that she kept in the trunk of her car. She kept a bottle of mouthwash up on a file cabinet in the back of the classroom. She claimed that she had a toothache all the time. I was naive at the time and didn't have a clue what was really going on with her. I never once smelled alcohol on her breath but knew something was wrong.

One Friday, the students as usual, were in an uproar when the time for recess came. I was grading papers for her in the back of the classroom, where she liked me to stay. I suppose she thought that I wouldn't smell the alcohol on her breath if she kept me in the back of the classroom. She let the students go outside and asked me to watch them while she went out to her car. Their play area was between our building and a building right across from us. Two students began fighting and ended up back inside the classroom with their fight. One pushed the other into my desk - which shifted the corner of my desk into my ribs - just as the teacher came back inside, too. By that time, the students were so unruly that she couldn't calm them down.

I could not believe what transpired next. The teacher sat down on an empty desktop in the front of the classroom, put her hands on her head and stated in a matter-of-fact tone of voice: "I'm going to bring my "two-twenty" in on Monday so y'all can watch me blow my brains out." At first, I thought I had not really heard her statement correctly. Yet, I knew that I had heard her clearly. I also knew that her statement could not be ignored. It was simply inappropriate and dangerous. Some of the students laughed loudly and shouted at her to bring the gun in and shoot herself. I gathered my wits and knew I had to report the incident to the administration. Violence was a frequent thing in the lives of many of these students. I could even picture any one of several students bringing a gun and assisting her on Monday. I could not be silent. If anything happened, I would be at fault for not intervening. Plus, I would have never gotten over the tragedy and the aftermath effects on the students, the school, and the neighborhood. I waited until the end of the school day, stopped by the office, and told them that I had to speak with the principal before I would return to the classroom on Monday.

Monday morning came and I stopped in the school office. The principal wasn't in, but the TIS (principal in training) was. She asked me to go on into the classroom and she would call for me and the teacher to meet with her in just a little while. I was very uncomfortable having to go back to the classroom. However, I found out that they needed me not only to help students but also to monitor the teacher. It wasn't long until a substitute for the teacher arrived, and we were called into the office. Mrs. N, the TIS explained to the teacher that I had brought up some serious charges and asked me to repeat what I told her had happened. When the teacher heard what I repeated she claimed not to remember what she had said and done. She then stated that I had taken it out of context! How do you take something like that out of context? If you don't remember what you said how do you think it was taken out of context? I repeated exactly word for word what she said on Friday. How bizarre that she would react this way. She was sent back to the classroom ahead of me. Mrs. N told me that everything would be OK and not to worry.

I went back to the classroom, wondering what would happen next. Nothing out of the ordinary happened for a time. Later, she was called back to the office. After lunch, she actually had the students working on some sentences that she had assigned them, and things were going well. Then she nonchalantly walked over to where I was standing and said to me, "You know, the same thing could happen to you some day." I wasn't sure if she meant that she would blow my head off or if someone would tell some bizarre tale on me. I had told the truth exactly. She knew it and she knew that I knew it. I had to report it; it was required. By law, I would have been held accountable if anything had occurred as a result of her actions. Plus, it was the right thing to do. She was dangerous. She went on to tell me that because of what I had said, she had been given a choice: "Go get counseling or get fired." She chose counseling and was given an assignment elsewhere. She was incompetent, and the children had been harmed enough.

The next day, a substitute teacher was in place until a new teacher could be hired. I didn't realize that he was a sub. He was nice and the kids liked him OK, but he allowed one student to run the classroom. She mocked us and did whatever she wanted to, which hindered a proper or even adequate learning environment. After the previous situation, I knew that neither I nor the children needed to go through another unfortunate experience. So, after a few days of this, I finally told him that if he didn't send her to the office I would leave. He told her to go to the office, and she slowly walked out the door. However, I noticed that he pulled a chair over and sat in the doorway. At first, I just thought he was making sure that she went straight to the office. Then, I heard talking between him and someone. It was then that I knew he hadn't made her go to the office. She was right outside in the hallway. I immediately picked up my things and walked to the office.

It didn't take long for the students to get their third and final teacher of the year. That was in January and many of the students were failing second grade. It was not their fault. They had not had an adequate chance to learn what they needed to. I am sure that the "first year" teacher had no real idea of what she was taking on. She was a great disciplinarian and motivator. With solid rules, regulations and routines, things began to change. The students had to adjust, and adjust they did. High expectations were set, and they met the challenge! It was like a miracle had happened. They were happy, felt safe and were praised for their accomplishments. The children who had always done their best were now thriving and feeling that they mattered. There was very little time for the others to misbehave, and they became successful, in spite of every negative thing they had endured for the first half of the school year. I was thrilled and couldn't have been more satisfied.

Although things had immensely improved, there were a couple of boys, one in particular, who tried us. One day I was working with a child who didn't want to listen to me and continued to be disrespectful. I am sure that he had given up on learning since he had gotten so far behind. The teacher immediately called his mother when she observed what he was doing. He got himself on the right track for the remainder of the day. The next day, he came into the classroom limping as he walked up to me. I asked him what was wrong with his leg. As he pulled his pants leg up, he said that his mama had beaten him with a broomstick. There were big whelps on him. I managed to keep calm, although I was shaking inside. I asked him why it had happened. What a stupid and unimportant question! He said it was because he had been so disrespectful to me the day before. I asked him to let me see his arms and back. He did. There were more whelps everywhere. I showed the teacher; she took him to the office and welfare services were notified. His mother was mortified with his behavior. She was like many others who didn't have the skills needed to deal with their children and went too far disciplining him. What a sad situation. I could not get the picture of his little beaten body out of my mind and cried like a baby that night. I felt guilty that he went through this because of how he had treated me. I wondered if there had been anything different that I could have done to help modify his behavior. Sadly, he was only one of many children who still go through similar circumstances.

The things I saw and heard are still heartbreaking to me today. I remember going home crying every day of my first year there. The circumstances were so bleak that I can remember feeling a pall throughout the building. When I was assigned to work with individual students and small groups at different times of the day, I had my work cut out for me. However, their teachers would inform me of their needs, and I was allowed to plan for them. They were significantly behind the others on their grade level. Some of the fifth graders couldn't write a complete sentence or write it correctly. Forget about them writing a paragraph. I had to backtrack to their level and bring them up. It was a very slow and tedious process.

One day as I was working with a group of about twelve students, I assigned them a writing exercise. I always came up with high-interest topics to get them motivated. Knowing that if they could not identify with a topic, there was no way for them to even begin writing about it. On that particular day I assigned the topic: "The Person who Means the Most to Me". As usual, I heard "I can't write." and "I don't know how." I worked hard to get them started, encouraging them with, "Yes, you can!" I told them that I had faith in them and knew that they could do anything if they wanted to do it bad enough. They kept giving excuses and I kept answering with reasons why they could accomplish the task. I would get blank stares, frowns, and more negative comments. I walked around the long table assisting each student by answering questions and giving them tips and ideas. At one point, I looked around and noticed my student who was always clowning around and disrupting us. He was a tall, thin student who never seemed to take things seriously, unless he was angry, and he would refuse to even try to work. Time and again,

I'd had to send him back to his classroom in order to be able to work with the other students.

This time, I saw huge tears running down the child's face. I was shocked since I had never seen that reaction from him before. I walked over to him and asked him what was wrong. He said that I had asked him to write about the person who meant the most to him. I agreed and asked him again what was wrong. With tears still running down his face, he told me that his mama was the person who meant the most to him. He went on to say that people were always making fun of her, and he didn't know how to write about it. My heart was touched to see how emotional this usually rowdy child was. I didn't know what this was all about. I didn't want to ask why but I asked, "You love your mama, right?" He replied, "Yes." Then I asked, "Your mama loves you, right?" He was sobbing at this point. "Yes," he replied. I told him to put his pencil down because he was too emotional to try to write. Later that day, I found out that his mother was in jail. What a heavy burden for a child to bear. I was extremely glad that I had empathized with him. I knew he needed someone to listen to him that day. He put his pencil and his head down and remained subdued for the remainder of the session. If I could have put my arms around him, I would have. After that day, I never had another problem with him. He continued to struggle but he attempted to do the work that I asked him to do, and without acting out or disrupting us.

There was a little boy who drew me to him and made a difference in my AmeriCorps® experience. Our teams were assigned by two of our leaders to come up with plans and implement a two-week summer day camp in the inner-city. We were not given much time to plan but we worked very hard in every spare moment. We planned and implemented the camp with gusto and guts. Everyone said we did a great job. The leaders were impressed. Now, the little fellow that attached himself to me was constantly into anything and everything that he could be. He was one of the youngest children and full of way too much energy. I figured that he was one of the babies who had been born with drugs in his system which his mother took while pregnant with him. He simply had to be moving; he could not sit still. He was constantly interrupting and asking question after question - whether the questions were appropriate at the time, or not. I took him under my wing and watched over him, trying to keep him out of trouble. I called his name many times to distract him or make sure he was doing the right thing. Then one day, he told me his name was Duke. Therefore, I began calling him Duke, much to his cousin's dislike. The cousin told me that his name wasn't Duke, to which I replied, "If he wants his name to be Duke, that's what I will call him." After all, it made him happy, and he grinned big. He was funny, mischievous, and very busy, along with hard work just trying to keep up with him. Duke disappeared for a while one day. When he saw Officer Cook, who was at the day camp with us, suddenly running after a suspect that she had been trying to find, Duke took off running after her. He knew her from working in the neighborhood and wanted to run with her. She kept telling Duke to go back inside the building with us. He had no idea that a criminal was involved. He either wanted to help her catch the perpetrator or just wanted to have fun. He was a kid of action and he certainly jumped into action that day. It could have ended in tragedy. I didn't let him out of my sight for the remainder of the camp. He was so tiny and cute, extremely curious and hyperactive enough to need several guardian angels to watch over him.

There was one member of another team who did not like me and made things as hard for me as she possibly could. I didn't like her either but tried to keep my distance. She was rude, hateful, and tried to bully me, for some reason unknown to me. Fortunately, we didn't have to work too closely together, except at the two-week camp. I volunteered to teach crafts to the children, and they eagerly worked on them. We divided the kids into small groups, having them rotate to different centers. On the last day of the week, I gathered all the materials out of the trunk of my 320-Z, took them into the building and set up my centers. Of course, we were very busy. I did not notice my keys missing until I packed my materials up at the end of the day. I looked around at all the places inside the building that I might have left my keys. I couldn't find them. I went out to my car and searched the ground around it. I looked through the windows to see if I had left them in the ignition or dropped them on the seat. They were nowhere. I fretted and went back inside to look again, asking everyone I saw, including the kids, if they had seen my keys anywhere. They all said they had not seen them. I continued to search inside. After about an hour of sheer frustration and panic, the member who totally despised me walked up to me. She was holding up my keys and asked if that was what I was looking for. I sighed and said yes, asking her where she had found them. She smiled and answering smugly said, "In your trunk early this morning." She had held onto my keys all day long and watched me frantically searching for them at the end of the day. Only when she was ready to go did she say anything to me. Everyone was appalled that she had the gall to do this. The area we were in was known for gangs and high crime. She very likely saved my car from getting stolen, but she didn't endear herself to me anymore than she had already.

There are many more stories that happened while working with AmeriCorps®. I'm thankful that I had the opportunity to work with this organization. It gave me a good picture of what I could expect when facing students as a teacher. They not only gave us the opportunity to learn but also gave us a stipend to help with our school expenses. I highly recommend them for those who want a worthwhile cause to work for.

A Few Special People: Some I Call Family

As you go through life, you have people that become come into your life and remain. Memories are made. Peggy was my neighbor and best friend. We lived on Walton Street in Pensacola, and we were more like sisters than friends. We played together; had sleepovers; went places together, and she helped me with my math homework. She helped me with my math homework so that we could play sooner in the afternoon. Mama and Grandmother had Peggy's mother make me the prettiest clothes. Most of them were made of taffeta material with tiny embroidered flowers. I was a tomboy but transformed into a prissy little girl when I wore those dresses.

One day we decided, along with some of the other neighborhood kids, to build a mini-amusement park for all of us to play in. There was construction on several new houses on the street. So we went around and gathered all the leftover materials that we thought would help us begin our project. We wanted to begin by building a mini ferris wheel. Now, we were so excited and couldn't wait to get our project underway. We were self-assured kids and had the confidence that we would make our amusement park happen.

As we began to nail the first boards together together, my granddaddy wandered over and asked us what we were doing. I'm sure that my grandmother had seen us and sent him over. Unfortunately, our hopes and dreams were shattered when he explained that our neighborhood wasn't zoned for an amusement park. If anyone else had given us the bad news, we would have probably just hidden the materials to try again when we thought no one was paying attention. But Granddaddy had a gentle way with words, and we would listen to him. We were disappointed but we took all the materials back to the properties we had gotten them from and forgot about our plans. We soon went on to some other plan like most kids do.

Peggy and I went to the local shopping center on Saturdays with Mama and Grandmother. Our favorite place to go was the lunch counter at Walgreens. We sat on the bar stools at the counter and ordered the same thing each time we went. The first time we ordered, the waitress got a good laugh. We didn't care. When she would see us coming in from then on, she'd smile and say, "One banana split with two spoons coming up!" We shared. My guess is that we did not have enough money for two banana splits, plus, we couldn't have eaten a whole one by ourselves. Peggy gave me my first camera for Christmas one year. I was in fifth grade and my love for taking pictures of anything and everything was born. I even took pictures of my dog and dolls sitting in "my classroom" as my students. I was always playing teacher. When Peggy got married, I was her flower girl. She was about three years older than me, and I was a small child - just the right size to be her flower girl.

My very first friend, Karen, and I recently reconnected on social media. Memories of us and our families are many. Our parents were good friends before Karen and I were born. One of the memories that we look back on and laugh about are the times that our mothers took us across the highway to the cemetery. We would feed the ducks and have a picnic. It was a beautiful cemetery and we had fun there. What fond memories. When my family moved out of state, Karen and I lost touch and we grieved for each other. I found her on social media about two years ago and was ecstatic. It was like we had never lost touch.

Penny was the second person that I met. She lived next door to my grandparents, and we became great friends. We lost touch for the same reason that Karen and I did. We, too, found each other on social media. One of my favorite memories is the day that Penny and I ate a dozen Easter eggs. Well, Easter eggs are yummy! Another time, I got us into big trouble. After school, we were going to the bus area, and I decided we would ride Rocky's bus home. All the girls, including me, had a crush on him. He was a handsome young bus driver. We could ride his bus because he drove along the same route, so what could it hurt? I convinced Penny to ride his bus. The problem was, when he got to a certain street, he asked Penny and I where our bus stop was. I told him that it was "just a little further." He looked puzzled and asked why we got on his bus. "Because we wanted to." We told him each time he asked that it was just a little further. Finally, Rocky said, "Look, this is as far as I can go." and we had to get off of his bus. Our families were getting concerned and looking for us by that time. I don't remember how far we had to walk but for two little girls, it was too far. We finally made it home and we never rode Rocky's bus again.

My grandparents sold their house to Cindy and Ginny G's family and Stephen, Ann, and Laura C. became like family when Mama took care of them while their parents worked. We all had fun times and created many great memories. Those childhood days are precious to look back on.

Ree, the twins - Shirley and Sheila, Janice, Janie and I were best friends in Jr. High and our first year in high school. We decided that after we grew up we would go into the fashion business together. Each of us would play a vital part in the company. When my family moved, that ended my part, and we went our separate ways. I lost touch with Janie, and Janice developed cancer and passed away after we were grown.

Ree got married and moved to Alabama with her husband and her artistic talents. For decades, every time a new president went into office, she drew a cartoon of him, and sent it to him at the White House. President Reagan and Ree corresponded throughout his presidency. He told Ree that her cartoon of him was his favorite and hung it right outside the Oval Office where anyone who came that way could enjoy it. Shirley and Sheila are artists, as well, and have many talents. Sheila is a caterer. I have seen pictures and heard about how delicious the dishes she creates are. Shirley works two part- time jobs that she loves.They both love the ocean and nature where we grew up and find themselves there often.

Cindy E. and I met on our first day of our junior year of high school. We had both decided to come out of our shyness and make new friends in a new school and new state. We sat in the first two seats in our homeroom class and chatted. I think that Cindy spoke first, and we knew we would become friends. Our families had similar backgrounds and we found we had a lot in common. Cindy was better at making friends than I was. I never got out of my shyness in the two years that I attended school there. I wanted to make friends, but I didn't know how. Many days, Cindy and I would walk to and from school together. We talked a lot about life and got to know each other well. Cindy introduced me to Debi and Marilyn, but it wasn't until social media came along that I reconnected and got to know a lot of the people from Hanahan High School from which we graduated.

After graduation, I got married and moved to Jacksonville, Florida. A year and a half later, Cindy got married and moved to Jacksonville, too. I had my first child, then Cindy had hers. I had my second child, then Cindy had hers. Our lives have been parallel for most of the time we have known each other. We have been through similar tough times and good times - and mostly at the same time. Cindy has always been there for me. We live in different states but only a little over two hours away and still have similar lives. Amazing!

I had challenges getting to school when I was endeavoring to earn my degree from the University of Florida. My car turned up missing and I had no transportation to travel forty-five minutes to an hour to get to class. I would catch buses and taxis to meet my car pool until it became too much. I called Cindy one afternoon and we caught up on each other's lives. It had been a while. Within a short while, she called me back and told me that she and her mother had talked and wanted me to come live with them so that I could finish school and get back on my feet. What a surprise and a blessing! My carpool ladies lived in the same area as Cindy did. It would now be easy for me and it would not inconvenience my carpool friends any longer. Cindy and her family were so good for me and good to me. They fed me, encouraged me, and did whatever they could for me. Her daughter helped me get my first teaching job at the charter school where she taught, teaching separately and then together, and sat on the Child Study team as the only two special needs teachers there. We got to know each other well. That gave Cindy and I another bond and she is like another sister to me. What a treasure!

Edith is another friend who has a lot in common with me. We began teaching at the same school as Special Needs teachers. We spent a lot of time commiserating and encouraging each other. We had to. It was not the best environment for either of us and we needed each other for support. Most of the Regular Ed teachers were good to us and we shared laughs and ideas with them. I also got to know Edith's family and found them to be very sweet and fun to be around. Edith has been through a lot of health challenges. She went into the girl's restroom to get a student back to class and fell, injuring her leg. There were complications. Because of this, she was diagnosed with a brain tumor. If she had not fallen and injured her leg, the tumor probably would not have been found. Because of that and my brain injury, we had even more in common. We were both changed in many ways. Yet, we survived!

In my early teaching years, I had two paraprofessionals who made teaching easy for me. They supported me and knew exactly what was needed to make the classroom run smoothly. I rarely had to ask them for help. They knew what was needed and stepped up to the plate, making me look great! Jessy was my first paraprofessional in Florida and Norma was my first paraprofessional in Georgia. We had some challenges dealing with some of the students but we supported each other and also had a lot of fun working together. It helped that we had a lot in common. We had very similar backgrounds. In addition, Anne was the first teacher I worked with in Georgia and Kacie and Sharon were in the classroom next door. We worked well together and encouraged each other. We also made it fun and bounced great ideas off each other that made us better at teaching.

While I was waiting for a teaching job in Perry, Georgia, I asked for a job in a small department store in town. I was ringing up purchases when a young mother and twin boys came to the register. I noticed their eyes first. I can't describe them accurately, but I could never forget them. They were beautiful. I asked the boys if they were shopping for school clothes and they told me they were, as they smiled excitedly. After a few days, I got a call from a private center to teach in the Pre-K program. When the day came for the students and parents to meet and greet, in they walked! I was so excited to see them again. Tammy, their mother, was a little nervous that her "babies" were beginning school. She was even more reluctant to have the boys in separate classrooms but they would be next door to each other. That worked out very well because they were able to spend time during the school day with other children and make new friends, until recess - when Austin and Jacob were pulled to each other like magnets. Then came the day when Jacob decided to play with some of his friends. Austin was in a state of incredible disbelief and panic. He followed Jacob all over the playground trying unsuccessfully to get him back as his sole playmate. His reaction was totally unexpected and took a long while to calm him down. It was quite an experience for everyone. When summer break came around, Tammy needed a sitter for the twins and I quickly took the job. The first day with the boys, Jacob got in my lap and Austin tried to pull him out of my lap saying, "She's **my** teacher!" I tried to explain that school was now out; I was there for both of them and it would be ok. It took a while to calm him down again that day. He thought that I belonged only to him. Whew! Tammy was a great resource and got me a job working in the GED program with prisoners in the jail in Macon and in some community centers. I left the family when my first grandchild was born and ended up staying for nearly two years. When I got back, Tammy had need for a sitter again. This time, there were two more children: Jordan and Owen. So there were four in all. Jordan was in school by this time and Owen was not quite three. He, Mama, and I would go to Waffle House for breakfast nearly every morning. We had a good time together, and there was never a dull moment with four boys! Austin and Jacob were continally trying to educate me on one subject, or another. They were funny. They have just graduated from different universities and Austin is married!

There are so many people who have been put into my life for one reason or another. I can't write about them all. However, I would be remiss if I didn't mention Drs. Mosetta and Leonard Cohen. Mosetta started me out on my teaching journey and saw me throughout the whole teaching preparation. I not only took three of her classes but I also worked as her assistant in the Social and Behavioral Sciences Department. She also headed our junior college program in AmeriCorps®. We became friends along the way, and I lived with her and Leonard for a while when I needed a place. They always made sure that I was well-fed and ok. They graciously gave of their time, talents, and wisdom, and taught me how to handle a lot of challenges. They encouraged me and others, as well, including my teammates Barbara (who graciously opened her home to us when we had to work on our projects), Stephen, and many others. I would not have had such a great educational experience without Mosetta. She tirelessly proofread all of my papers in my last term at the university. I was exhausted and under a lot of stress. She gave me ideas that helped me get started on my last project when my mind went blank and refused to work. Once she helped me get started, I was able to get through it with flying colors. She and Leonard were always ready and willing to lend a hand and help me when I needed anything at all. I will forever be grateful. I haven't been able to see them in far too long but we keep in touch. I consider them family.

Linda and Debbie were ladies that I met in a class we attended in college. We realized that we needed help with our struggles with algebra. So, we would meet regularly and work our way through the tough subject. We took several classes together, studied and encouraged each other. We studied together at school and in restaurants that welcomed students. We shared our challenges as students, mothers, and life in general. We enjoyed many times together and learned from each other. Susan and I met at church. She lived in St. Augustine and drove up to Jacksonville on Sundays. She is always encouraging me, in spite of all she has been through. She is very thoughtful and sends cards and books to me. Iris and I met online through a website we were on at the same times and got to know each other. She is a writer and very inspirational. Her life story is incredibly amazing. I mentioned Connie, my pen pal and getting to finally meet in person. There's Debbie, whose grandmother was my fourth grade teacher. Also, Pat who has been a friend I have been able to lean on in some tough times. She knows.

Finally, I think of my classmates that helped and encouraged me during some challenging times - my classmates in our journey to get our degree in teaching. Rosalyn, affectionately called Roz, and the youngest of the group, was always my project partner. She is sweet, funny, and we worked very well together, producing "A" grades. Tammy, Lynn, Sam, Debi, Tina and everyone in the cohort were always ready to encourage and lend a hand to each other. My carpool classmates went above and beyond for me. Margaret and Karen went out of their way to make sure I had a ride to school when I no longer had my own transportation. They were always making sure I was OK. Karen offered me a place to stay with her and her children so that I could attend the last term of our program. I ended up living with my friend Cindy and her family, as I mentioned. At the end of our program, Margaret gave me a tiny, beautiful guardian angel wind chime and told me that since they wouldn't be near enough to watch over me any longer, that the little angel would always remind me that I was loved. What a sweet and thoughtful gift she gave me. I will always treasure it and the reason for it.

I have always been incredibly blessed throughout my lifetime with the people that have come into my life. There have been too many to mention and not enough time or space to write it all down. However, I hold each of them in my heart and am thankful for them and everything they have brought into my life. I hope that I have been a blessing to each of them. I don't believe in coincidence, but I believe that there is a reason for people and things that come my way.

In Spite of it All

Well into the first practicum (Student Teaching) for my degree in Special Education, we had a student who, usually sweet, had a meltdown and the teacher put her in the time-out room for isolation. Our department was located in a wing away from the Regular Ed students in the school. We had children who had severe emotional disorders and were subject to have huge outbursts. Each room in the L-shaped wing had a time-out room which had block walls with a small window for observation.

When this student was put in the time-out room, she became substantially angrier and her behavior escalated. She began kicking the door to the point that we couldn't carry on with the lesson adequately. She was kicking so hard that the sound reverberated throughout the classroom. She knew that the other students couldn't hear. I decided that if I put my foot against the door, it would muffle the sound and we could continue. She only kicked the door harder.

After about fifteen minutes, I felt a sharp pain go through my foot and could no longer muffle the sound with my foot. I moved my foot and the student had to be removed and sent to the intervention room, which we didn't like to do because they were given pity and allowed to talk, which was against the policy. The pain in my foot subsided and I was able to go on with the job at hand. I forgot about the pain. That was on a Friday afternoon.

I was scheduled to return the rental car that I was driving. The drive was lengthy in rush hour, so I stopped at a convenience store. Coming out of the store, I didn't realize that the sidewalk where I stepped came together at a ninety-degree angle. My foot slipped down onto the pavement, barely tapping it. Tremendous pain shot through my foot, and I heard what sounded similar to a pencil break. I had to sit down on the sidewalk because I was in so much pain that I became extremely nauseated. The owner came rushing out of the store and yanked me up. He told me that I was OK and helped me hobble to my car. He roughly helped me get behind the wheel of the car and I somehow drove to the car rental company. I had to use my left foot instead of my right foot to maneuver the gas and brake pedals. My right foot was in too much pain.

I got to the car rental agency and turned in the car. I rented another one because I needed to get to the hospital to get my foot checked. I also had to work and then be able to get to the University of Florida for class on Saturday week. My foot kept swelling and the pain was intense as I drove to the hospital. I didn't think about calling an ambulance. I knew my foot was broken and X rays confirmed it. The metatarsal bone - one of the tiny bones - was broken. Since it was Friday night, there was no one available to put a real cast on it so they put a temporary cast on to help me get through the weekend. They also gave me crutches to use because I wasn't supposed to put my weight on the foot. I had a hard time balancing on the crutches and told the ER doctor I didn't think I could use them. He told me quickly that I'd get used to them.

On Monday, I was able to see a bone specialist and had a real cast fitted from my toes to my knee. I was given instructions on how to take care of the cast and to come back in a few weeks. When I went back to work on Tuesday, the child who had first cracked the bone by kicking on the door was shocked to see me in a cast and asked me what had happened. I didn't tell her about the final break on the sidewalk but remembering the original searing pain from her kicking the door, I told her she had broken it. She had fractured it, making the final break easy to happen. She was so apologetic, but I told her that I didn't want to talk to her. She acted pitiful and remorseful all day long and kept begging me to forgive her. I already had but wanted her to understand the consequences of her actions. When the day was coming to an end, she asked me once more to forgive her and not tell her father. She was down on her knees. I told her that I forgave her, and she would need to remember what can happen when we let our temper get the best of us. She said she would never act like that again. The next time she decided to act out, I pointed to my cast, and she calmed down.

Saturday came and I had to drive to Gainesville for class, which was about an hour and a half drive. Another car pulled in front of me in busy traffic and I forgot about my foot and slammed on the breaks to avoid hitting them. The pain seared through my foot, but I had a class to attend. The class was a special class and wouldn't be repeated. When I arrived, my classmates were alarmed at seeing the cast on my foot and asked me about it. I explained everything.

We had a break at some point during the morning session and I left the classroom alone and started down the breezeway to the restroom. As I neared the halfway mark, I got too close to a brick column and my right crutch got caught in the mortar between two bricks. Snatching the crutch several times to get it loose, it wouldn't budge until the last time I snatched it. I lost my balance and fell back on my broken foot. Not only was the pain intense but also my pride was in more pain. I was a student in my fifties and here were young students conversing and seeing me. I was mortified. A young man came over and asked me if I was OK and began to help me get up. I was grateful to him. I could not get up by myself. He was a sweet young man. I finally made it to the restroom and saw that my eyebrow and eyelid had turned a dark purple color and swollen twice its size. As I started out of the restroom, a classmate caught up with me and we talked as we walked back to the classroom. She noticed that I didn't turn my head her way, so she turned to get a better look at me and gasped, "What happened to you?" Then, she laughed nervously and said that they couldn't trust me to go to the restroom alone and that they were going to go everywhere with me from then on.

I had started classes in the beginning of the program with Mononucleosis and they'd seen how sick I was. I didn't know what was wrong for a while, but I knew I was quite ill. My classmates began to be very protective of me, for which I was grateful they cared that much. I would go through many other challenges before graduation and it felt comforting to know that the ladies had my back, so to speak. They were a great group, sacrificing their time when I needed rides back and forth to classes, and encouraging me through some tough times. I didn't live close to them, yet they provided what I needed. In spite of it all, I made it to graduation. I will be forever grateful to these ladies with hearts as big as the world.

Oops!

There are times when you just need to think before you act, as I often told my students. I learned this the hard way, not once, but many times. I was a slow learner in that department. One of those times was the morning I walked to school with my cousins. I should have thought and used common sense, but I was determined that I could do anything they could do.

It had been raining, resulting in puddles on the ground where we had to walk. That one puddle that Terry, who was tall, just stepped right over it. Dollie, who wasn't quite as tall as Terry, jumped over the puddle. I was the short one. Of course, I jumped and landed right in the middle of the puddle, messing me and my clothes up. What a mess I was and had to continue to school. We didn't have cell phones back in 1971. I was so embarrassed. When we got to school, I used the office phone to call home for clean clothes and the day was saved. My pride wasn't!

Then, there was the time when I was grown and went to have my hair done. I parked my car in the parking lot. Sherry was the best hairdresser I ever had. I first went to her when she was a new professional. She worked in the hair salon in a department store. After a while, she moved on to another beauty salon. I followed her. Then she opened her own salon. I followed her wherever she was because she knew exactly how to handle my difficult hair better than any other beautician had. She worked miracles with my hair.

I don't remember how long I was in the salon, but my hair looked good after Sherry finished with it, as usual. I paid at the counter and went out the door. I stopped quickly on the sidewalk. There, in the middle of the aisle sat my car! I ran. Hurrying to unlock the door, I quickly got into the car and saw that I had neither put the parking brake on, nor had I put the car in park! I wish I could say that it slipped on its own, but I am sure I failed to think clearly. The thought occurred to me that, if I had not finished in the salon when I did, my car could have rolled into another car, or person, and I would have had a big problem. It could have been a life and death matter. That was the last time I did that!

Among many other various incidents, was the time when I rushed to get ready for a funeral. The funeral service had been in progress for a few minutes when Renee looked down and noticed that my shoes didn't match. I had gotten dressed in a hurry, and when I went to grab my shoes, I grabbed two black shoes, not noticing they didn't match. Renee and Mama laughed at me all during the funeral and never let me forget about it.

There are times that I hope everyone, and not just me, have been in a hurry; loaded the car; gotten in, and driven off with something they had put on top of the car because they needed to free up their hand to unlock the car door. I have done this many times. I have left my camera, my Bible, and a cup full of drink on top, among other things. Sometimes, someone will see it and let you know. Other times, you just drive off and you lose the camera. Somehow, I remembered my Bible before I lost it. I have lost cups, and who knows, maybe I have lost other things and never remembered I had them!

I think maybe I will do more silly things from time to time. The older I get, the harder it is to remember things. Hopefully, it won't get too serious. I hope I can always look back at my memories, smile, and even laugh at myself. Maybe the sad memories will be few, and the bad memories will fade. Maybe I will grow more positive and focus less on the negative.

Christmas Eve Blessing

It was Christmas 1989. It was to be a Christmas to remember. First, we were to travel from Jacksonville, Florida to Moultrie, Georgia to celebrate Uncle George and Aunt Daisy's surprise 50th wedding anniversary dinner. We had to return home that night, since Lenny had to work that evening, and we would leave the next morning to go up to Perry, Georgia for Christmas with my family. It was going to be the best Christmas ever and we were looking forward to it.

It so happened that someone looked out of the window at the end of the anniversary dinner and saw the magic of snowflakes falling. What a beautiful sight it was! It was an evening of joy and happiness. The snow made the evening more special for our dear Uncle George and Aunt Daisy. They were such a special and loving couple and were always a joy to be with. The snow was unexpected, and we were all thrilled to see the evening end this way.

Renee left with Roy's parents because she didn't want to travel back home and then backtrack in the morning. She was too excited to get to my grandmother's place. A lot of relatives would already be there, and she didn't want to miss anything.

My parents and grandparents had always treated her special and she knew a good time was waiting. I remember thinking as we left the restaurant that I wished Lenny had not had to work that night so that we could all go on to Perry together.

As we traveled, snow began to fall harder and faster. We turned on the radio for weather reports, only to hear that some of the major bridges in Jacksonville were going to be closed early. Panic set in for me. There we were without both of our children and we had to get back home to Lenny. We called him and found out that he was home because the pizza store closed early, due to weather conditions. He was home alone. What if the electricity went off and he was cold or hungry?

The road conditions got worse, and a usually 3-hour trip took us 8 hours. We had to drive slowly. We were from the south and were not used to icy roads and bridges. We saw accident after accident - with cars driving into overpass bridges. It was frightening. All I could think of was that we had to get home and back to have both of our children together with the rest of the family. After all, this was the night before Christmas Eve, and if we didn't get home and back up to Georgia, we would be without our children on Christmas. Renee would have no gifts under the tree in Perry, and Lenny would be alone at home. Well, that had never happened before, and it couldn't happen now!

The weather reports continued with more road and bridge closures, and we weren't sure how we would reach home. But to reach home, we must. After the long night, we found one bridge still open. The Main Street Bridge was the only way we could reach home, and we traveled slowly and carefully across it. We finally got home safely. However, we still had to get back up to Georgia in a few hours. It was Christmas Eve. We had to. We just had to. We just couldn't be separated from Renee and the family for Christmas.

After a few hours of sleep, we found that we could travel the back roads if we were careful and get to Perry. We borrowed my father-in-law's suburban because we felt that it would be a safer vehicle to travel in. Plus, we had a lot to carry up to Perry and it would fit better in the suburban than in our car. Snow and ice lay on the ground, so we had a quick snowball fight before we loaded ourselves into the suburban. It was silly in view of the situation but fun and relieved a lot of tension. Then, we began our Christmas trip. We were all feeling much better and ready to begin our Christmas celebrations.

Forty miles out of Jacksonville, in Folkston, Georgia, the axle broke on the suburban. We were stuck in the middle of nowhere. We were able to slowly get into the parking lot of Jack's Convenience Store. Now what were we going to do? Folkston is a small town. There were no motels and no car rental companies. No repair shops were in sight. But even if there were, it was Christmas Eve and they weren't open. We used the pay phone to call the Highway Patrol and told them where we were. They said that they would come to see about us to make sure we were safe, but they couldn't promise they could do much to help us.

We waited about two hours and the Highway Patrol finally showed up. It just happened that there were two Jack's stores at either end of the county. They had gone to the end of the county - opposite where we were - and couldn't find us. It began to get late, and I knew I had to call my family to let them know what had happened, but we were OK. When my brothers and Daddy found out where we were, they said they were coming to get us. I told them we were over three hours away and the roads were bad. They didn't let that stop them. The Highway Patrol told us that there was a repair shop a few miles up the road and we could have the vehicle towed there. We told my brother where we were going to be towed, and we would wait there for them to come after us. As soon as we got off the phone, they got into the car to come after us.

The owner of the repair shop towed us and the suburban to

his place and we all got out. He started walking over to his house, not knowing how long it would take for us to be picked up. There we stood, out in the icy elements and I knew we would freeze to death. I called out to him, asking him if there was a place we could wait inside until we were picked up. He told us he had a small office at the back of the property with a small space heater where we could wait, so we walked carefully across the ice to the office. He turned the heater and TV on for us. He also pointed to a small trailer next door and told us that his son and family, the Davis's lived there. He told us we would be welcome to stay over there if we wanted to. I told him that we didn't want to intrude on Christmas Eve and thanked him for letting us stay in the office. He again said that they wouldn't mind us waiting with them, and if we changed our minds, to go on over, and he left.

After about an hour, the temperature had dropped even more, and the little space heater was not enough to keep us warm. Our feet were getting too cold, and we decided to go over to the little trailer to stay until we were picked up. How I disliked barging in on a family on Christmas Eve. It seemed too much to ask. We had no choice. We walked up to the door and knocked. The door was opened by a young woman and a very bouncy two-year-old. We explained why we were there and were graciously welcomed in.

One moment was all it took to see there was no Christmas preparation going on in this little family's home. No Christmas tree, no gifts anywhere, and no aroma of anything being baked or cooked. I felt sadness wash over me. We were invited to sit down and make ourselves at home. Two-year-old Jessica was so excited to have someone to entertain. Entertain, she did. She was very sweet and looked like a little angel to me. There was also a baby boy on a blanket that rolled a little too close to the heater from time to time. The men began a conversation and so did the young mother and I. Jessica began to engage Lenny with her antics and chatter. In no time, the question that had burned inside of me was answered by the young mother - which was why were we there, instead of on our way to our family?

Her exact words were, "I know why y'all are here. We needed someone to visit us tonight." She began to pour her heart out to me, explaining that she had run away from home, and had gotten pregnant, and was deserted by the baby's father. She then met the young man sitting at the table who married her. Jessica wasn't his, but he appeared to love her as his own. After they were married, they got pregnant with the little boy. She went on to say that they had no transportation except for the tow truck. We talked for over two hours and my heart went out to this family who had next to nothing. Yet, they welcomed us with open arms and hearts. There I sat, in my nice warm clothes and thick jacket. We would have more than we needed on Christmas. I felt guilty that I had it so good.

Daddy and my brothers arrived, and we left, hugging this sweet little family, and telling them that we would return after the suburban was repaired. They told us that they were so glad that we had come and told us to hurry back.

We got to Perry sometime in the early morning hours and everyone was relieved that we were there, and safe. The next morning, we got up and had a wonderful Christmas celebration, and way too much food. However, my mind continued to wander back to that little family in Folkston. I told our story, and everyone was deeply touched. We knew the suburban would be ready in a couple of days, and we were going to take as much food to the couple as we could. Mother looked around the house and picked out some things that could be used as gifts for all of them.

Grandmother was especially touched and cried when I told the story and how we had been welcomed. She wanted to meet them personally, but she wasn't able to travel. Little did we know that this would be her last Christmas. I remember feeling the love and concern in her heart for that little family who had saved our lives. I think it was the best part of that Christmas for her. She talked about how kind they were. They had nothing. Yet, they gave us their hearts, friendship and trust, beautiful memories, and saved our lives. It was a humbling experience.

When we returned to get the suburban, we unloaded all the food and gifts we had brought. Little Jessica was bouncing all over again. We had a big variety of food and a gallon of milk for them. The young father looked as if he couldn't believe his eyes and the mother began to cry. She said, "I can't believe this! How did you know we didn't have any money to buy food and milk for the babies?" My mind was overwhelmed, and my heart wanted to break. That was even more reason that the accident happened. We needed to feed and show this family love.

We spent as much time with them as we could and headed back home. It was hard to leave, but it felt good to know that we could do something small for them after they had saved our lives. Sadly, we lost touch with them after a while, but on Christmas, I remember them and wonder how they are. I hope to find them again one day. I hope they are doing well and that they have never been hungry again. Yes, it was a special Christmas Eve blessing.

Mental Whiplash

We have all had those "What?" moments in life. Those are times when we are simply flabbergasted. Sometimes, these are funny moments. Other times, these are "I don't believe this!" moments. There are several incidents that come to my mind.

When I was in Junior High school, I knew a girl who was frequently borrowing lunch money from me. She had older sisters who wouldn't listen to her because they said that she had already been given lunch money at home. No one seemed to know what she had done with her lunch money. However, she knew I was a softie and didn't want her to be hungry. During the course of the school year, she borrowed quite a bit of money from me. When I asked her when she was going to pay me back, she would say she didn't have it. I repeatedly asked her to pay me back. Her reply was always the same, until one day when I asked her for the money, she replied, "I'm saving my money!" When I called her during the summer to tell her that my family was moving out of town, she asked, "Gail, who?" I told her and she claimed not to remember me. I suppose that she thought I was going to ask her for my money. I was so perturbed by that. I told her to go get her yearbook and look me up. Then, I slammed the phone down.

As a young child, I greatly admired the pastor of our church. He and his family were good people. I thought so much of him that I wanted to give him a gift of something he would always remember me by. So, one Sunday morning, I was standing at the door of the church waiting for him with my gift in hand. When he came up to the door, I told him to hold out his hand. He did and I handed him my prized possession - a handful of Roly-Poly bugs! He was very puzzled! I was so proud of myself for giving him something I treasured. I can still see the look on his face. It was a look of utter surprise and I thought I'd pleased him. Therefore, I reached my goal.

Then, there was the time that my son, Lenny told me that he had an entry in a show at the mall. He had made something in Metal Shop and it had won a ribbon. I was excited and rushed to see what it was. While looking around, I saw marvelous iron works of shelves, planters, gun racks and more. I saw beautiful work on display but couldn't find Lenny's entry. I asked the teacher where it was. He told me that it was in the enclosed glass case. Eagerly, I walked over to see my talented son's masterpiece. All at once, I saw it. It was finely crafted and I was stunned. I stood there, letting it sink in. It was a perfect replica of Freddy Krueger's glove. Lenny loved horror films and books, so that is what he chose to create. I survived that shock in a few days.

This is the same child who joined the band and practiced his trumpet every day. When Mama and my kids came to pick me up from the bank where I worked, Lenny and his trumpet leaned out of the car window and practiced faithfully. I hope the bank employees and customers enjoyed it. He also brought the neighborhood kids in while I was taking a bath one time. He said he had an important question. I yelled, "Out now!" They all ran out giggling. I was not amused. I had forgotten to lock the door.

There were "What?" moments with Renee as well. When she

was about 4 or 5, she went to see my grandparents with my parents. Daddy loved the way the town barber cut his hair, and he would stop there. Mama and Renee went into a children's clothing store, and they saw a beautiful dress that Renee fell in love with and had to have. Mama told her it was out of the question because it cost 80 bucks. She flew out of the clothing store and into the barber shop. Running up to Daddy, she said, "Andy, quick! I need 80 bucks!" (The grandchildren called Daddy Andy.) I made the dress for her, and she was just as happy. This same child was 3 years old when she was found in the water hose on the first cold snap of the year. When I asked her why she was in the water - and with only her underwear on - she seriously answered, "I was dirty!" Three-year-olds are interesting.

In addition, there was the time after Renee was seriously ill in the hospital. She had to have blood transfusions to replace all the blood she had lost and continued to lose before they figured it out and got her back on the road to begin healing. After two weeks, she was back in school with a lot of catching up to do. She had written a letter to our mayor at the time, Tommy Hazouri. She admired him and wanted him to know. He was coming to visit her elementary school to talk to the students. Since she had been so sick, and was having a lot of adjustments in her life, I wanted to cheer her up. I called his office and asked the lady who answered the phone to request that he meet her in person at the assembly. Sure enough, at the end of his speech, he called her up to the stage; shook her hand and told her that he was proud of her for being very brave during her illness. I was thrilled, thinking she would be smiling from ear to ear. She never cracked a smile. She shook his extended hand and came back to her seat. I asked why she didn't smile or say anything. Her reply was, "He's just a normal man."

There were Saturday mornings when I could sleep late. My children would come running in - sometimes bouncing on my bed, and ask if they could watch cartoons. I would always tell them yes. This happened over and over again. Finally, I told them on a Friday that they could watch cartoons and they didn't have to wake me up to ask. The next morning, like clockwork, they ran in. This time, they whispered, "Mommy, can we watch cartoons?" I sleepily replied, "Whispering also wakes Mommy up".

Everyone has probably had at least one automobile accident in their life. As for me, I went through a period of over two, maybe three years, when, every three to six months, someone would hit the back of my car. It wouldn't have happened any more frequently than if I had a sign on my car with a target that said, "Hit me!" On the day that I was released from weeks of therapy, I was rear-ended by a teacher. Back to weeks of more therapy. Another day, I was sitting at the window of a fast-food place. The window where you paid and got your food was, for some unknown reason to me, on an incline. I was rear-ended by a lady behind me. Still another day, I had traveled home from Georgia to Florida to attend a meeting. I was sitting at a traffic light near a busy intersection when all of a sudden, the car behind me was rear-ended, hitting me, In turn, I rear-ended the car in front of me. Then, it happened again! We had no place to pull over so we had to go up an overpass and to a parking lot in a small shopping center. We started up the overpass. The next thing I remember was waking up on the overpass, with someone beating on my window asking me if I was alright. Next, I realized that I had gotten to the parking lot without remembering how I had gotten there. A teenage male came up to my window at that point apologizing, and begging me not to call the police. He explained that he was driving his step-father's car, without permission or driver's license. Of course, he wasn't insured. There were many witnesses and the other drivers involved. Someone had already called the police. Oh, sweet therapy. I'm back again. That was the second craziest time I was hit.

The craziest time was when I was sitting at another traffic light. The mall was on my left. So was a young man with a nice truck. All of a sudden, he pulled across three lanes, and got in between me and the vehicle behind me. BAM! The guy jumped out of his truck cursing at me. I asked him why he had hit me. He angrily shouted, "Well, no one would let me in!" "So, you hit me?" I asked him. He loudly spewed more choice words at me. "I just put a $1,000 bumper on the front of my truck today!" I calmly reminded him that he was the one who hit me, and that I was just sitting in my lane, minding my own business.

We all have our memories. Sometimes, we are able to look back and laugh at them. Other times, we continue shaking our heads in disbelief. These moments will come. Mine have come rather frequently and I could have done without the events that I recall. It is "mental whiplash", the quirks that life throws at you!

From Fear to Security

Most of the time, the things we worry about never happen. We worry for nothing. Sometimes, the things we worry about do happen and catch us off-guard, even though we are worried about them. The latter was the case when I had my worst week teaching. I had some extremely difficult students and paperwork galore. I was exhausted and ready to regroup over the weekend. It was going to be a great weekend.

It was the Friday before Mother's Day and my parents had come to town. They were at my brother's waiting for me to come home from work. I was very glad to be getting near home and starting our weekend visit. My little house was a former parsonage that I rented from the church on the property. It felt safe, and I couldn't wait to get home to my safe abode after the week I had.

As I rounded the corner of my street, the first thing I saw was three police cars. Two were in my driveway and the third one was in my yard. I couldn't believe my eyes and the stress that I was feeling increased to a much higher level. I parked my car on the street, and a police officer came walking over to me, and asked if I lived there. I said yes, and he told me that my house had been broken into. They thought they still heard someone inside and the canine unit was on its way.

My heart sank and crazy thoughts went through my mind. Although I knew that my parents were at my brother's, I imagined that they had come over, and Daddy had run to do an errand, leaving Mama there to rest. Maybe she had been hurt in the break-in. I was shaken to the core. I was irrational and was imagining many things, even though I knew the police were there to catch them if they were still there and would make sure I was safe.

Soon, the canine unit arrived, and the beautiful police dog was taken all around and inside the house. The burglars had escaped and quickly. The police found that they had taken the AC window unit out of my bedroom window and entered the house that way. Since the alarm went off, the police were there in a minute and a half. The thieves didn't have a lot of time to snatch and grab. They knew what they were looking for, and took coins out of my dresser drawer that I was saving for my kids and I. It amounted to quite a bit for me but it wouldn't make them rich, by any means. I had no jewelry or anything of great value, so they had to be disappointed. I had no drugs for them to take. The only thing I had of any value was my computer. They only missed it because the police got there so quickly.

I used my cellphone to call and check on my parents. They came right over when I told them what had happened. I was shaken to the core and felt violated. Strangers had been in my house and taken the liberty to plunder through my personal belongings, taking what they had time to take. My parents slept in my bedroom while there. I couldn't even think about sleeping where strangers had come in. I slept in the living room, and there I slept for about six months. I would shake, thinking that I had to sleep in my bedroom. The police told me after the break-in that they didn't want to frighten me, but that when burglars don't get everything they want, they usually come back. That surely frightened me. I had seen an ad previously about a "mechanical dog", which was a motion activated speaker, and would sound off in a vicious dog's bark and frighten burglars away. Searching the internet, I found one and ordered it. When it came, I plugged it in and activated it. I felt much safer. However, it only covered motion for a 90-degree area, and I was still afraid to sleep in my bedroom.

Finally, I toyed with the idea of getting a live dog. I did not want to be tied down with the responsibility of a pet so I thought long and hard until the idea of being a sitting duck for criminals won. I decided to get a rescue dog and took a look at the local Humane Society. I didn't want a big dog or a really small dog, but a dog with a big bark would be ideal. After walking around the cages three times, I still didn't see what I wanted.

However, I noticed that each time I got to one cage on the end, a small dog with big brown eyes kept looking at me, as if he were pleading with me to take him out. I couldn't even tell what kind of dog he was, and he didn't look like he would be a good protector. Yet, his eyes kept calling me. The lady that showed me around told me that this little dog would be perfect for me, since he was a miniature Schnauzer-terrier mix. Schnauzers are very protective and usually a one-person dog, meaning that he would be loyal to me only. I thought that was a good idea. But I still wasn't exactly sure if he was right for me in other ways.

He wanted me to take him out of the cage, and when I couldn't while making the rounds with the lady, I noticed that he sadly went over and lay down with very sad eyes. That got to me. Because his eyes kept calling me, I begin to think that he was the dog for me. I sat down and talked to him for a while. When I got back to the office and told the lady that he was the dog I wanted, she was thrilled but told me that there were at least five other people who wanted him and I would have to wait and see if they fell off the list for one reason, or another. I was hopeful but I figured that he would go to someone else. He had picked me, however, so I went back to visit him three days in a row.

On the third day, he was mine! Everyone else had lost him for various reasons, I was told. I knew it was meant to be. He was mine, and I was his. After they got him processed, I adopted him. Rascal and I excitedly left the building. We were both ecstatic. He was jumping all around, and I was smiling big. When I opened the car door, he jumped right in as if he knew where he was going. I talked to him all the way home and told him that I was happy to be his new owner so that he would feel safe with me. I had no worries; he owned me, as it turned out.

I had to be very careful with him. The lady at the Humane Society told me that he had been very abused and that he was a runner. A runner he was, and I couldn't let him off his leash when we were outside. I also had to be careful when I opened a door to make sure he didn't get out when he wasn't supposed to. I had to chase him several times to get him back when I first got him. I couldn't scold him in a bad tone because it would terrify him, and he would cower down, and cover his head or get under the bed.

I made the decision to rename Rascal and he was already acting like my little Buddy. So, I repeated the name Buddy frequently to get him used to his new name. Sometimes, I would call him Rascal Buddy to associate him with his new name. It worked, and he responded to his new name pretty quickly. Buddy, it was, and he would prove to be the best little buddy that I had in a long time. He would definitely show how good and how protective he would be in the coming months. He wouldn't let anyone near me.

Now, at that time, I wasn't working and kept looking for a job in two cities. I intended to take the first job that was offered to me because I had been driving back and forth from Jacksonville, Fl. to Perry, Ga. to visit my parents weekly and wanted to get back to work as soon as I could. After I adopted Buddy, I packed the car, bought the few things I would need for him, and we headed up to Perry. When we got there, my parents weren't home but they returned in less than an hour. When we headed into the house, Buddy ran in, and landed in Mama's lap before she barely got seated on the sofa! The lady at the Humane Society told me that he was a lap dog. He certainly was. If he wasn't sitting on my lap, he was on Mama's, unless we were eating, taking him for a walk or a ride on the golf cart.

We were to learn soon that Buddy was afraid of men and children. It took him a long time to begin to warm up to Daddy. He never accepted but one child, and he learned to love some of our female friends. He finally warmed up to Daddy when they went on early morning walks. He would growl and snarl at first but Daddy showed no fear. Buddy finally learned to love Daddy very much as time went by. On the morning that Daddy died, Mama found Buddy sitting in front of the door with his leash he had chewed into from trying so hard to get us to Daddy. It was a sweet but sad sight. Mama and I told him that he had done a good job taking care of Daddy. He wagged his tail as if he knew he had gotten Daddy home, and he didn't leave him alone. After Daddy's funeral, Buddy's instincts took him over to the gravesite each time we walked over to the cemetery. It was amazing - the bond they had. Buddy had not one person he was loyal to. He was loyal to me and Mama, too. He was also a faithful dog, even though Mama had spoiled him rotten!

Special Meetings

I never thought I would ever meet anyone that was considered a VIP in my life-time. It could be considered a novel idea. There may be times when you actually meet an interesting person that many people have heard about in the news or otherwise. You never forget where you were and how you met; what they were really like in person; and if you were pleased that they were the people you thought they were. I have had the privilege of meeting four people that I will never forget.

The first time I met someone considered important, was when I was a young girl working at a department store in the credit card division. I answered the phones, along with several others, when shoppers wanted to charge something on their store credit account. We would look at their file and if they had enough credit, we would give credit approval. Sometimes, we had to decline the charge. We filed the charge and credit slips daily for previous transactions.

This particular day, I had gone to lunch and when I returned, the other credit clerks told me I had missed a celebrity. I asked who it was. They told me it was Bob Barker, the game show host on TV. They said he had come to see our boss who he had been longtime friends with. I didn't believe them. There was always someone coming up to our department to pay their bill in person. There were some interesting people who came in. I thought they were trying to play a trick on me. So, they told me to go down the hallway to the conference room and I would see for myself. I did but felt real silly. When I got close to the conference room, I heard talking but couldn't hear what they were saying. I peeked around the corner and there sat my boss and Bob Barker. He was in one of his brightly colored blazers. He saw me and winked. I'm sure that I blushed. I hurriedly backed away and went back to work. The girls laughed and asked if I believed them now. I'm sure that he was used to silly young girls like me, gawking at him!

The second time, I was at a future teacher's conference. The Keynote Speaker was Grace Corrigan, Christa McAuliffe's mother. Christa was the teacher who was to fly into space on the Challenger Space Shuttle. History was being written. Sadly, the shuttle exploded under two minutes after liftoff. Mrs. Corrigan's purpose was to talk to future teachers about keeping Christa's dream and legacy alive. I thought that she would have an entourage of bodyguards and such to protect her. I thought she should. However, there were only a couple of people with her. After listening to her speak that day, I realized that she was true to her name. She gave a great speech and Christa would have been proud. She was as graceful as her name and a beautiful lady. She posed for pictures with those of us who wanted our pictures made with her afterwards and answered our questions.

The last two people I got the chance to meet were because of my daughter, Renee. She invited Mama and I to go with her to Plains, Georgia to hear President Jimmy Carter teach his Sunday School class. He did this at different intervals, and it wasn't always on the schedule. Mama and I were happy to go. We would also get to meet him, and First Lady, Rosalynn Carter after Sunday School and have our picture taken with them outside the church.

As we turned into the driveway of the church, we were met by security and their dogs, who sniffed all around and under the car. We were then directed where to park. We parked and walked up the sidewalk to a table that was right before the entrance to the church. There, they looked at the contents of our handbags and moved the wand all around us to make sure that we had no weapons and such. There were certain things that were not allowed inside the church.

We proved not to be dangerous and were directed to our seats. Before Sunday School began, we were given long, exact instructions, and rules by an interesting lady who had known the Carters and probably everyone in Plains all her life. The main thing that I remember the most was her saying words to the effect of, "Whatever you do, don't even think about touching either one of the Carters. If you even lay a finger on the President, Mrs. Carter will get hold of you, and Security will take you down!"

President Carter did a great job teaching Sunday School. He knew the scriptures well and was a very good teacher. First Lady Rosalyn was very pretty and such an elegant lady. When Sunday School was over, we stood in line with our cameras to have our pictures taken with them. It was pretty special to meet them in person. They were down to earth and welcoming. Mrs. Carter told me it was so nice to have us there and for us to come back soon.

All the people I met were very down to earth, friendly, and gracious. With as many people as they meet on a daily basis, I am sure that they get tired. They have to get frustrated sometimes with certain personalities and deal with them day in and day out. I am sure they have days that they just would like to cancel all their appointments and hide. After all, they are humans, like us.

Decline of a Mind

ementia. I let it sink in when the nurse told me that was what Mama had. Dementia! No! Not my mother! Daddy had it first. He was put on medications that they thought slowed his down. Mama's wasn't that recognizable to me for a long time. I just thought she was grieving for Daddy and her sister and was doing a lot of strange things. She was grieving. She began to lose her balance and fall. The falls continued, and became more frequent. She had had knee replacements and had very limited movement in them. Therefore, she could not get up by herself.

Also, it was difficult, and sometimes impossible for me to help her get back up. I would be able to lift her up about three feet. Then, she would stiffen and tell me to put her back down because she didn't want me to hurt my back. She knew that I had a bad back but what hurt the most was when she stiffened and put more strain on me. Sometimes, I could pull a chair over and lift her enough to sit on the edge of the chair and pull her over to the sofa. She could slide onto the sofa once she was on the chair.

One day, she fell near the front door. I couldn't get her up, no matter how hard I tried. I told her that I had to call 911 for help. She became so upset that I continued to try to get her up, to no avail. The front door was open, and a friend and neighbor heard the commotion and came to see what was going on. I was so happy to see Kay. Kay can do anything. She told me to go get a bed sheet. I did and she showed me how to use it to lift Mama. Why did I not think of that? By that time, Mama was falling up to three times a day.

After Daddy passed away, I would put the trash can out by the street to be picked up the next morning. I would have to spray the inside with bleach to keep the raccoons out or they would turn it over, feast, and leave a big mess in the street. One night, I was sitting at the computer for a while when I realized that Mama had left the room. I went to look for her downstairs, then I searched upstairs and I searched again. She wasn't to be found. It occurred to me that she must have gone outside. I couldn't imagine why. It was dark and I started to panic. I opened the door and she was yelling for me. There she was. She had fallen into the street in front of the trash can. "Mama! What are you doing out here?" She yelled, "I've been calling you for an hour!" (We had been talking less than an hour earlier, but it was too long for her to be outside by herself - at night, and lying in the street!) I asked her again what she was doing out by herself. She told me she was tending to the trash. "Mama!" I told her I had taken care of it before dark like I always did. I don't remember how I got her up that time, but I probably pulled the golf cart around. It wasn't as hard to get her onto it.

Shortly, we planned to travel to be at my first grandson's birth. Mama got very sick. We'd planned on both of us going but I took her to the doctor, and she was hospitalized with the flu and pneumonia. She told me to go on, that she would be in good hands. Plus, friends checked on her for me and my brother and his family came into town to stay with her. My grandson was born with a hole in his lungs and had to be transported to the NICU in the children's hospital a few miles away. It looked as if we would lose him. We were given no hope. He pulled through in a few days, thankfully.

Meanwhile, my siblings knew that I couldn't make the decision to put Mama in the nursing home. I knew it was best for her, but I struggled with guilt. She had always taken care of everyone else, and I felt that it was my job to take care of her now. I finally admitted that I couldn't take care of her any longer and she would be taken good care of by the nursing home staff. After my grand baby got put into Step-Down, I came home to get Mama and things she would need at the nursing home. She went willingly but thought it would only be for a short while. That was one of the hardest days of my life. I had to return to my daughter's the next day. I went by to see Mama and explained that I would be back in a few days, since she was better. She was cheerful and upbeat. I cried all three hours back.

Mama continued to get better physically. In her usual way, she thrived in the nursing home. She knew a lot of people there, since she had visited them for several years. Some of her own friends became residents, and she made new friends as well. She seemed to be fine but continued to fall. She was adamant that she would not use a walker or a cane. She had been self-sufficient and was walking up to eight miles per day before she got sick. However, I began to notice that her thinking wasn't as clear as I thought it had been. She was getting things mixed up and telling me things that didn't add up. She was certain that she was right. I was not happy with the attending physician at the nursing home because he wouldn't answer my questions adequately. It was hard to know when he would be there, and I was getting frustrated because I felt Mama could be better. I got her an appointment with a neurologist. I was desperate for help and answers. Plus, I was tired of hearing that it was her age. But this was Mama! I had to get any help I could for her. She was put on medications for dementia. After some time, we could see that she continued to deteriorate and was taken off those medications. It went into Alzheimer's.

When characteristic delusions and hallucinations occurred, it was cruel for me. But I had to learn not to let my anxiety show in front of her. I already knew that you shouldn't argue or get upset with an Alzheimer's patient. It would upset them too much. The delusions and hallucinations are real to them. It was real to Mama. When she thought Daddy was visiting her, it was a blessing to her. When she thought that I had been a part of her childhood, it was confusing to me at first. As time went on, I never knew which decade she would be in but I went along with her. I answered her questions as well as I could. At first, when she would ask about Daddy, I would remind her that he had suddenly passed away that cold early January morning. She would say, "Oh, that's right. I forgot." Her countenance would drop, and we wouldn't talk until she was ready. It was cruel for both of us. When she thought that Daddy had visited her, it was a blessing to her. She and Daddy were best friends and loved each other deeply.

Mama went through so many stages and changes. There were times that she would tell me that she was getting married. That was very distressing for me. People made jokes about it which was very hurtful to me. I knew she had no clue what was going on and that "boyfriends" didn't exist. My daddy was the love of her life and she was lonely and back in her teenage years. It was cruel to have to see her in another world and it was a blessing that Daddy didn't have to see her deteriorate. He would have understood because he was a very perceptive person. But watching her become like a child would have been cruel.

At the same time, when she remembered something that made her happy, it was a blessing to her. It took me a long time to reach that point, but I learned to be happy when she was. When she cracked an unexpected joke, and seemed to be in the present day, it was a blessing to both of us. I finally learned to laugh at some of her ridiculous antics that had earlier made me cringe and want to cry. Getting that far, however slowly, was a blessing. It was much easier to laugh than cry. Besides, I knew it wasn't Mama - but the cruel disease.

It was cruel that I slowly lost my mama, my friend and confidant. Yet, she confided in me and knew me almost all the way to the end of her life, except three times. That was and still is a blessing. Many times, I wasn't sure what she was talking about as she progressed deeper into the dark world of Alzheimer's. Other times, I was able to decipher at least some of it, and help solve some real problems for her. That was a blessing.

It was a blessing when she was able to participate in activities at the nursing home. It was cruel as she declined and lost interest, mobility, and the mental capacity to participate in anything. It was cruel to us both that the Covid Pandemic happened, and I couldn't visit her for much too long. For a while, we could talk over the phone; Covid put an end to that. She had become unable to call and answer her phone. Not being able to hear her voice was depressing.

It was a blessing that we had Mama for a long time, 94 years. While thankful for that, she is sorely missed. There are times that I need to talk with her; hear her voice and see her face to face. Mama was a blessing to far more people on this earth than just our family. Mama was a second mother and friend to anyone who needed her in her time before Alzheimer's took her away from us. She was strong, courageous, and knew a lot more than I will ever know. One doctor told her he didn't know why she was asking him so many questions, that she knew more than he did! She read and learned on her own. She was curious about things in general and soaked up knowledge like a sponge. Alzheimer's is a sad and cruel disease. It will be a blessing when they find a cure.

Mama survived colon and breast cancer. However, she couldn't survive Alzheimer's. I never thought anything could ever be stronger than Mama. However, she is no longer sick and in pain. She is in Heaven with Jesus, family, and friends. That is definitely a blessing.

Now What?

I lost my firstborn, my son, suddenly and unexpectedly in December 2023. He was sweet, funny, and loyal. In addition, he was talented. My life is forever changed and sometimes it just stands still like it is frozen. At other times, I think he is going to call, or text. Then, I remember. He is gone and I think my heart will burst from the reality. I have yet to work through it. I may never fully come to terms with losing him. Still, there are many memories which bring comfort to me and many that bring a smile. Losing him is my worst dream, come true. I should have gone first. I should have been there as he took his last breath. The last time we talked was on his 50th birthday and we didn't get to finish our conversation. He called a couple of days later but I didn't hear the phone ring. I didn't know he had called until I saw it on my call log several days later. Then came Monika's phone call that he was gone. He had one of his migraines and she let him rest, not knowing he would soon be gone. Monika found him when she went back to check on him a little later. He was happy with her - they were the perfect couple. She is alone now after 22 years with him.

My voice mail stays full and I have been told to empty it so more messages can be left. Not yet. As much as I want to hear my dear son's sweet voice, I am not ready. When I feel stronger I will listen and save his messages. My dear sweet son, my heart hurts. Neither my head, nor my heart wants to believe you are gone. I know we will meet after I leave this earth behind. There is nothing harder than losing your child. It is a pain like no other. If you have lost a child, you understand. If you haven't, I hope you never experience the loss.

To make it even worse, someone impersonated him on social media about a day after he died and sent friend requests to me and several friends. How cruel. I have reported them and asked that they be removed. So far, the person is still active. It hurts.

Thankfully, I still have my talented daughter and three loving grandchildren. My older brother died early one Christmas morning after he had been seriously ill for a long time. I have his family, my sister, my younger brother and their families. However, I don't get to see them very often. Funerals of family members are the only times that we have been able to see each other for the last few years. We text, call, and stay in touch on social media but it isn't the same as seeing each other in person. Still, I know they are there, however far away we are in miles. They are talented, fun, and hold a special place in my heart. My sister taught me a lot, including how to crochet. We all loved to play pranks on each other. Their spouses put up with us somehow. In addition, my younger brother and I went clowning together. We were always up to something. My nephews and neices are great and I was with Brandon and Jacob nearly every day when they were little. They called me "Mommy, too" sometimes. When I moved out of state, I was sad that I couldn't see them as much. Since Mama and my son passed away, I haven't been in much contact with friends, except on social media, and that has been a lot less. In time, that may change. I actually called a cousin and two friends this week.

I could write more about a lot of people, family, friends,

places, and things; however, it would likely take many years to complete, if ever. My story isn't over - not even close. I have been very blessed. For that, I am thankful. I am thankful for my faith and for God allowing me to live a full life. He is always with me. Finally, I am thankful for a certain American Film Critic, who found out that I had a manuscript - which just sat, not going anywhere. He asked me when I was going to get it published. Mr. J.K.C., here it is, finally!